الاخوة الاعزاء ...
أرجو قبول هذا الكتاب
اهديكم مع محبتي وتقديري

موقع سالم ازايم
نسخة ١٨/٩/...

Men Who Dream, Can Do

Men Who Dream, Can Do

A Memoir by
GEORGE ZAKHEM

QUARTET

First published in 2009 by
Quartet Books Limited
A member of the Namara Group
27 Goodge Street, London W1T 2LD

Copyright © George Zakhem 2009

The right of George Zakhem to be identified
as the author of this work has been asserted
by him in accordance with the
Copyright, Designs and Patents Act, 1988

All rights reserved.
No part of this book may be reproduced in
any form or by any means without prior
written permission from the publisher

A catalogue record for this book
is available from the British Library

ISBN   978 0 7043 7165 1

Typeset by Antony Gray
Printed and bound in Great Britain by
T J International Ltd, Padstow, Cornwall

CONTENTS

	Foreword	9
1	Recollections of my Childhood	13
2	Parents	34
3	The University Years	43
4	The Start of My Working Life in Pakistan	58
5	The Beginnings of an Independent Professional Career in Lebanon	77
6	The Founding of Zakhem Engineers	100
7	The Challenges of Arbitration and the Blessings of Parenthood	115
8	Crisis, Success and Honour	130
9	Diversification and Investments	151
10	My Family	156
11	Social and Philanthropic Work	163
12	Towards Retirement	185
	Acknowledgements	195

For my parents,
SALIM AND HANNEH,
who taught me that love, hard work,
and honesty are their own reward.

FOREWORD

I have often wondered whether I should write the story of my life. Taking such a decision has weighed heavily on my mind. My wife, Lisa, and my two sons, Salim and Marwan, influenced my thinking on this matter and helped me to begin writing this memoir. They have always been fascinated by the stories I tell of my childhood in the village of Deddeh, Lebanon, and how my parents strove to provide their family with the basic necessities of life during the Second World War.

Obtaining an education during the time when I was ready to enter school was quite difficult – almost impossible – because there was only one elementary school in the whole of our district (Al Koura, Lebanon). This school was located in Bishmizene, some twelve kilometres from Deddeh. To acquire a basic education, starting at age seven, I had to walk for approximately two hours with my mother and elder brother, Antoine, along footpaths and trails through the green fields and olive groves to Bishmizene. My subsequent secondary and university education was no less challenging.

My professional life has now spanned more than half a century, yet I am still working as enthusiastically as ever, although my circumstances have changed considerably since I began my engineering career in 1955 in Doha, Qatar. Sitting amid the comfort of the living room in my London flat in late 2004, I could see the famous Hyde Park on one side, the imposing Royal Albert Hall with the Prince Albert Memorial on the other, and from the terrace on the south side the extended campus of London's Imperial College. On the western terrace of my flat, two olive trees from Lebanon, each about ten feet high, stood flourishing as a reminder of my roots and all that I had experienced during my lifetime. As I reflected on the path my life had taken, it occurred to me I could not have dreamt that one day I would be living in the United Kingdom, in my own home in the centre of a great world metropolis.

As I sat listening to the steady hum of London traffic, my mind began to wander back in recollection of past memories: the early struggles to acquire an education; working my way through university; the thrill of graduation; the first jobs in faraway places to make my mark as an engineer; establishing my own business; the satisfaction of seeing the Zakhem firm develop; and, finally, the opportunity to pay my debt to the country of my birth and give back a little of what I have received over the years from Lebanon, the land that I love.

I do not recall for how long I sat reminiscing, but it must have been for a considerable period of time. Images of years gone by passed rapidly through my mind. I remembered the sacrifices and love of my parents, and the vivid memory of my mother carrying my books on her shoulder and taking my brother and me by the hand during our daily two-hour walk from Deddeh to school at Bishmizene. I also remembered the people who had left an indelible mark on my life, and one by one I counted my blessings. As the shades of an autumn evening began to fall, I took the decision to write this book to express my gratitude to my parents, my dear wife, my family, and my friends and colleagues for the part they have played in helping me on my way to achieve success.

Beyond recording fond memories, I hope that this book will help those who are about to set out on the path of life to understand that if they have drive, tenacity, honesty, dedication, and faith in themselves they will certainly succeed in accomplishing their goals.

إني رأيت أنه لا يكتب إنسانٌ كتابًا في يومه إلا قال في غده: لو غير هذا لكان أحسن، ولو زيد كذا لكان يستحسن ولو قدم هذا لكان أفضل، ولو ترك هذا لكان أجمل، وهذا من أعظم العبر. وهو دليلٌ على استيلاء النقص على جملة البشر.

—العماد الاصفهاني

For I have found that if a man were to write a book today he would on the morrow say: 'If this phrase were to be changed it would be better; if this other phrase were to be added it would improve the text; if this statement were introduced earlier it would be preferable, while if this other were omitted the text would be more beautiful.' In this reconsideration of one's work lies a great moral, and it is further proof that all men are imperfect.

Al-'Imad al-Isfahani (Editor)

CHAPTER 1

Recollections of my Childhood

I was born in 1935 in Deddeh, a village in the north of Lebanon about ten kilometres from the city of Tripoli and five kilometres from the Mediterranean seashore. Tripoli is the second largest city in Lebanon and in the 1940s it had a population of approximately 60,000.

In contrast, in my home village of Deddeh (located in the district of Al Koura) there lived about 3,000 people. Al Koura was notable, however, for two reasons: first, it boasted the highest percentage of educated people in Lebanon; and second, its inhabitants produced the best olive oil in the land. Sitting on a hill that rises 300 metres above sea level, the village commanded an excellent view of the Mediterranean Sea from the west. From the east, one could also see the High Mountain of the Cedars of Lebanon. It is connected with Tripoli City and the neighbouring villages of Fih and Batroumine by stone and gravel roads. As there were no automobiles at the time, people travelled on foot, or rode donkeys, mules, and horses. Basic infrastructure such as running water, electricity, telephones, and a postal service did not exist in those days. Water for drinking and domestic use was obtained from underground wells filled during the winter by draining rainfall from the roofs of houses and other buildings. Kerosene lamps of different shapes and sizes provided illumination at night. In short, a simple way of life prevailed in Deddeh.

From childhood, my siblings and I were taught by our parents to help others in our community, especially those who were less fortunate. I was no more than ten years old when my mother asked me to dedicate two hours a day during my vacations to teach other children how to read and write. This was during the Second World War and the years that followed. There were many children in our village who could not afford to attend any school. There were no public schools and the private ones were very few and expensive.

Children who sought some rudimentary instruction used to sit around my eldest brother, Antoine, and me as we instructed them using a home-made blackboard.

In spite of her heavy household burdens, my mother always found time to assist other housewives to get through a sickness or childbirth. My mother's aunt was the only midwife in the village, and my mother assisted with deliveries and follow-up care. In some cases my mother tailored clothing for new-borns and performed other tasks to benefit needy families.

My parents were devoted Christians who professed the Greek Orthodox faith associated with the Church of Antioch. The Greek Orthodox Church has a religious tradition with certain unifying principles and attributes. Under regimes that tolerated it and under those that persecuted it, the Greek Orthodox community has withstood the vicissitudes of time. Conflict within the religion itself and between its multiple patriarchates has not shaken the fundamental structure of its unity. Instead, it has imbued the community with a sense of resilience. Despite a significant decrease in the community's population and a loss of political power in the Middle East in the twentieth century, members of the Greek Orthodox community have played, and continue to play, an important role in the region today as catalysts of dialogue, as educators, scientists, doctors, and businessmen.

The Greek Orthodox community is a prosperous and well-educated entity, and many adherents have distinguished themselves in the field of politics, culture, and literature. Mikhail Naimy, for example, is one of the most illustrious names in modern Arabic literature. He has also achieved distinction in his English writings, especially his *The Book of Mirdad*, a mystical work of universal appeal. Others include: Charles Malik and his contribution to the Human Rights charter, Michel Aflaq (Ba'ath leader in Syria); Charles Debbas (the first President of Lebanon); Antoun Saadeh (founder of the Syrian Social Nationalist Party); and Jurji Zaydun (novelist).

The Greek Orthodox Church has faced a number of challenges, but its ability to sustain itself for centuries in the Middle East has made it one of the most well-established religious institutions in the region. While the Greek Orthodox community is not the only Christian minority, and there is an underlying unity connecting all Orthodox Christians, it is entirely separate from the other denominations. Orthodox Christianity is permeated by the spirit of St John Chrysostom. In the Greek Orthodox tradition, emphasis is placed on the concept of the 'whole man', and on love, liberty, co-existence, and faith in God which is expressed through sacrifices in His name, obedience to His word, and devotion to the Virgin Mary. The fact that only a small fraction of its members attend church regularly is not because of a lack of belief, but because the Greek Orthodox view religion as something which encompasses every aspect of life. Rather than designating Sunday as the only day for its celebration, the Church is actively and consistently lived through everyday behaviour, conduct, and social relations. Furthermore, the Greek Orthodox is one of the few communities which have been able to adjust to changing circumstances and new situations due to its members' steadfast and unwavering faith, determination, and devotion.

We attended church services on Sundays and applied the teachings of the Bible in the course of our daily lives. My father expressed his faith, in part, by joining the church choir. He would also walk for hours to another village to attend funeral services for people unknown to him. When asked why he took all this trouble to attend the funeral of someone he never knew, his answer was that it was the Christian thing to do, and that he wanted to give comfort to the souls of the deceased and their families.

We were raised in an environment in which the people of the community loved and respected each other. To this day I am mindful and concerned about those who work for me and I listen carefully to what they say about their personal and professional problems. Even during the first five years of my working life as an employee with private companies, I assisted my parents and siblings financially. During the first decade as head of my own company, I assisted my community by providing employment to a number of people from the village. Our employees were given the opportunity to learn a trade, such as welding, which allowed them to better themselves and their families.

* * *

I think I was six years old when I became fully aware of life and the environment that surrounded me. During the Second World War, a group of Australian officers who were part of the Allied forces stationed in Lebanon commandeered the upper floor of my family's house, which consisted of one living room and two bedrooms. Eight members of my family – my grandmother; parents; three brothers: Antoine, Ibrahim, and Albert; and two sisters: Najibah and Georgette – were confined to the ground floor of our house, which comprised one large room, built out of stone in the mid-nineteenth century. The ceiling was formed by two arches rising from the four corners to cross each other in the centre at a point six metres high above the floor, a traditional form of construction before the advent of cement.

The Australian officers who were billeted in our house spoke the first words of English I ever heard, albeit with an Australian accent. I remember my mother trading fresh eggs and other food with them in exchange for tea and butter. In general, the Australians were very kind and maintained good relations with our family as well as others in our village. They helped by supplying us with food like canned beef and milk, and gave us medical supplies such as aspirin and first aid kits. We were also given toothbrushes and toothpaste, and instructed how to use them. In addition, the villagers of Deddeh, including my family, learned a few English words such as 'good morning' and 'Merry Christmas'.

My grandmother, Tarfa, had been widowed shortly after her marriage. Her husband, my grandfather Tannous, had emigrated to Brazil around 1912, just two years before the beginning of the First World War. Tannous left for South America to escape the misery of living under Ottoman rule. He hoped to provide his family with a better life in the New World. He died in 1918 during a great epidemic that swept through Brazil, and so left behind my grandmother and three children: one girl and two boys. My father, Salim, was the second child in the family. He had no memory of his father and grew up with his sister and brother fatherless.

My mother, Hanneh, was born in 1914. She lost her mother, Najibah, at the age of six and she lived with a stepmother when my grandfather, Abdallah, remarried and his second wife, Jamila, gave birth to seven daughters and one son. My mother lived in a large family until she married my father in 1931. Both of my parents, then, had suffered greatly during their childhood, and knew the deprivations associated with the First World War and its aftermath. This meant that my mother was deprived of the love and tenderness of her mother, and my father was deprived of the security, firmness, and care of his father. My mother hardly knew how to read and write because her stepmother never sent her to school. My father, however, could read, write, and do simple arithmetic.

Both of my parents began working during their early teens to help support their families. My mother performed household duties such as cleaning, washing, and cooking. She also learned how to sew, a skill she practised her entire life. I remember how she made our clothes on a small Singer sewing machine placed on a floor mat in the middle of a room. She tailored clothes for every member of her family, including for my grandmother Tarfa (who lived with us until she died in 1958). My mother's sewing abilities knew no bounds; she sewed shirts, trousers, dresses, and underwear. She respected and loved her father, Abdallah, and he was keen to have his shirts and trousers tailored by her.

In addition to sewing clothes, my mother had to do all the household work and also raise a family of five boys and three girls. Providing food on a daily basis was a major preoccupation. Most of our family's food supplies came from a garden behind our house. This garden produced a variety of vegetables and fruits such as tomatoes, cabbages, cucumbers, potatoes, figs, grapes, and almonds. We had a sheep that gave us milk and chickens that produced eggs. My grandmother helped my mother to do her housework. In the same way, we children pitched in whenever we could, especially on school holidays. We hoped to reduce the burden on my mother as much as possible.

During the early part of the summer of 1943, I climbed an old peach tree in front of our house to eat some of its fruit. The branch I was standing on collapsed under me and I fell to the ground. As a result, I suffered serious cuts to my upper lip and nose. As blood gushed all over my face, I remember how worried my mother was. She wrapped my face in a cloth and immediately took me to the only doctor in the area who was in the nearby village of Batroumine, about half an hour away by donkey. We arrived at the doctor's residence at midday, but he had already left on his horse to make his daily rounds to nearby villages. The doctor's wife suggested that we await his return, which was scheduled for late afternoon. I lay down on my back on a couch as my mother tried to comfort me. Sometime around 5:00 p.m., my father was told what had happened to me and he immediately came to look for us at the doctor's house. When my father arrived, my mother and I both went outside. At that moment, two Australian soldiers who were passing by the doctor's house saw my condition. Showing great concern, they immediately took me to an army clinic, which was located in a big tent nearby.

At the Australian army clinic I received treatment and was cured in about two weeks. Everyone who knew my family thought that I was quite lucky because if the local doctor had treated me – so they said – I would have ended up with a deformed face.

This story about my injury shows how there was no medical help available in our village. If someone fell ill they had to be taken to the city of Tripoli, or else a doctor had to be sent for from elsewhere. People who were very sick were taken to a hospital in Tripoli by cart.

I remember how, at the age of eleven, I was learning to ride a bicycle in our village churchyard. I lost my balance when I hit a stone and fell off the bicycle. During the accident, my right leg was broken about halfway between my knee and ankle. I managed to stand up on my left leg. A moment later, my uncle Ibrahim, who had seen me fall, rushed up, scolded, and slapped me. Then, when he realised that I had broken my leg, he apologised profusely, kissed me, and carried me home on his back.

The next day my father brought two shepherds from nearby villages who were skilled at treating broken legs because they had experience caring for injured sheep. I was in severe pain, which the shepherds eased by massaging my swollen leg with hot water for about an hour. Then, the shepherds took a mixture of egg yolk and flour pasted on a piece of white cloth and wrapped it around my leg after fixing the bone in the proper place. This was a form of plaster.

Eleven days later, I was able to stand up and walk around by leaning on a stick. After about one month, I had completely recovered and could walk about normally. According to an old folk belief of my village, the healing period in days equals the number of years of the patient's age. That calculation worked for me, at least in this case: I was eleven years old, and was able to walk again with the help of a walking stick after eleven days of recuperation.

To earn money to support his family, my father opened a grocery shop. This shop was the only one of its kind in the village. To transport the goods he had bought from Tripoli, my father bought a cart and mule which he drove between Tripoli and our village on a daily basis. Every day at dawn, except Sunday, my father left our house with his cart and mule. The trip to Tripoli took about one and a half hours. By midday, he arrived back in our village with a cart full of goods. While my father made the trip to and from Tripoli, my mother ran the shop. On school holidays, my siblings and I helped out, mainly by keeping records of what customers bought on credit. Settlement of outstanding accounts was done on a monthly basis. My father accepted payment in cash and also in barter, such as fresh eggs and olive oil.

My father managed his shop in this way until 1948, when he decided to expand his business by buying a truck. He purchased this truck from the Allied forces that were still stationed in Lebanon. At this time, these foreign forces were in the process of withdrawing from the country. Now that he had a truck to transport his goods, my father began buying olive oil and olive seeds from sellers in our village and resold these items to merchants in Tripoli.

Our village was well known for the lime it produced. Local sellers used an old fashioned method: they created a wood fire in a cylindrical pit sealed on all sides with limestone. After five days of continuous fire, limestone was transformed into lime (CaO), a product used to produce mortar for the construction industry. Thanks to this production in our village, my father also began to buy and resell lime.

In my home village of Deddeh, there lived both Christians and Muslims. About two thirds of the people were Christian and one third Muslim. Deddeh had one church and one mosque. I remember how the Christians of our village visited the local mosque on special occasions, such as the Muslim Feast of Ramadan. I also recall how, as children, we imitated the *muezzin* performing the call to prayer from the mosque's minaret. Similarly, Muslim children attended our church on certain special occasions like marriage ceremonies and funerals.

Other mixed Christian-Muslim activities included our local volleyball team, which had five players from the Zakhem family and one from a Muslim family called Al Ayoubi. As we toured among the local villages playing other teams, we started calling one member of our group named Mohammed Al Ayoubi by the nickname 'Mohammed Al Khoury' after our local priest. In short, such excellent relations between the Christians and Muslims of Deddeh were a regular feature of life and both communities got on well together.

Obtaining an education – outside of what one learned at home – was beyond consideration because Deddeh had no school, nor did a single school exist in our entire district. The question of how to obtain an education for their children, however, was a constant concern of my parents. They discussed this matter whenever we gathered together as a family, especially for our evening meal. The situation seemed hopeless until, in September 1942, my father announced that his friend George Ibrahim Abdallah was opening a school at Bishmizene, a village some twelve kilometres away from our home. My father proudly stated that he had registered my oldest brother, Antoine, and myself at the school. We were to start classes at the beginning of October.

My parents placed a special trust in our school's headmaster, George Ibrahim Abdallah, who hailed from the nearby village of Fih. When I was seven years old, my mother walked my brother and me to school every Monday morning at 6:00 a.m. We reached our school about two hours later. We would spend Monday night through Thursday night with our aunt Mhabbi, who lived near our school. On Friday afternoon, my mother would return to take us back on foot to our village of Deddeh.

To make the journey between Bishmizene and Deddeh we traversed footpaths and fields of rugged terrain. We would carry our books, food, and other belongings we needed for the week on our backs and shoulders. Inevitably, my mother carried many of our items for us.

I always looked forward to these walks. Six decades later, I still remember vividly the terrain we crossed as we walked to school. I recall the valleys, rocky hills, and olive groves that went on as far as the eye could see. My brother and I could identify the kinds of trees we encountered along the way, and we counted the number of valleys and brooks we crossed on our journey.

It is with some nostalgia that I remember those walks to and from school, especially because my mother would tell us stories as we walked along. Her stories were related to our life or the life of those in our community. We were anxious to learn and we asked many questions, and my mother always answered even the most difficult of our queries.

One tale my mother told us was about an elderly man who lost all his teeth while walking across a valley called Wadi Kouwa, which was located about halfway between Deddeh and Bishmizene. As he was crossing the valley at night, some menacing fairies emerged from caves; they held rocks and were going to beat him. According to the story, the old man ended up having his teeth pulled out by the fairies. Properly warned not to wander about at night, my brother and I were always careful to cross Wadi Kouwa only during daylight hours!

One Sunday night before one of our trips to school, my mother Hanneh asked my grandmother Tarfa to wake her up early – at dawn when the 'Morning Star' appeared in the sky – so that we could start our journey early. The following morning, my grandmother called out to my mother: 'Wake up, Hanneh! It's time to move, I can see the Morning Star bright in the sky signalling the breaking of dawn. Please get the boys ready and start moving so that they won't be late for school.'

Soon my mother, brother, and I started to walk towards Bishmizene carrying our books and lunch. It was dark and we were walking close to each other. My mother was in the middle and rested her hands on our shoulders, thus giving us the security and protection that is so comforting when one is young. One hour later we still could not observe the dawn in the sky and we were getting very close to Wadi Kouwa. As we approached the Wadi, my mother said, 'Let's sit down beside this rock and rest for a moment and wait for dawn to break.' We pressed my mother to tell us about the fairies of the Wadi and asked if they would harm us in the dark. She calmed us by saying that no harm would touch us because we would not move again until daylight. When dawn finally broke, we crossed the Wadi and continued on our way, arriving at Bishmizene at sunrise.

By sheer coincidence we met the headmaster of the school, who was on his way to welcome the students. He was surprised to see us and called out in a loud voice, 'Hanneh, are you coming from Deddeh now, and alone?'

My mother answered, 'Yes, because as you know, my husband

Salim has to go to work early and I have to get the children to school on time.'

'Hanneh,' he said, 'I'm so proud of you and Salim. Children who have such parents are very fortunate; may God bless you all.'

At my school a tradition was established that every day before entering their classrooms, students would stand in a line, each class in its own row, and listen to a brief address by the headmaster or one of the teachers. That morning, Headmaster George Ibrahim Abdallah took the stand and delivered a speech about my brother and me, stressing how we had walked for two hours from Deddeh to come to school. He pointed out that we had arrived on time, while some students who lived only next door had arrived late. 'In life one has to work hard and persevere in order to achieve, and what I saw this morning from Hanneh and her children bears witness to this fact. I hope that what I've said today shall be a lesson to all of you.'

* * *

In 1944, Headmaster Abdallah left to open a school at another village called Aba. Because of his loyalty to his friend, my father moved us from the school at Bishmizene and sent us – together with our third brother Abdallah – to the school at Aba. Except for the three months of winter, we used to commute daily to our new school on foot, walking two hours each way between our village and Aba.

On our walks to Aba we were accompanied by other students from our village, all of whom were older than we were. I still remember the names of some of our classmates: Matta Khalil Matta, Michel Simaan Zakhem, Emile Hanna Kobrosi, George Hanna Kobrosi, Elias Simaan Lakkis, Abdallah Isa, and Edward Hanna Kobrosi.

As a group, we would leave Deddeh at 6:00 a.m. every day and reach the school at Aba around 8:00 a.m. The trip was both challenging and amusing. At the halfway point, we would sit down and have our breakfast. We would locate a rock – relatively flat and round on top – which we used as our 'table'. We sat around it, each one on a stone for a stool, and ate our breakfast. Our mothers had prepared our meals and packed them in a piece of cloth placed in a bag. We carried these bags on our backs, together with our books.

We took care not to linger over breakfast for too long so that we would arrive at school on time.

Classes would normally run from 8:00 a.m. to noon and then resume at 1:00 p.m. until 4:00 or 5:00 p.m., depending on the class. Lunch break was a time of real excitement because in good weather we used to disappear six or seven to a group and sit under the olive trees in the fields that surrounded our school.

We schoolchildren identified the seasons of the year according to the fruits that we ate. Walking daily to school across the rugged land and through olive groves and green fields that grew wheat and barley brought us very close to nature. It was autumn when we smelt the scent of olives and olive oil; winter when we ate citrus fruits; and spring when we ate green vegetables and observed the blossom on the almond, apple, and peach trees. During the summer we had all kinds of fruits such as grapes, figs, pears, and melons. All these products were grown on the land surrounding our village. It was a tradition that all families in the village should have an ample supply of such products, whether they grew them or not. Therefore, those fortunate in having enough supplies of such food were sure to give some to those who were less well off.

At the end of the school day, at about 5:00 p.m., we would all walk back to our village, Deddeh. On the way, we had to pass through two other villages, Bedubba and Batroumine. This journey was amusing because students who came from these villages joined us and we chatted with each other as we walked along.

My brothers and I would arrive home around 7:00 p.m., have our dinner, and do our homework before going to sleep at around 10:00 p.m. My parents would discuss our daily school activities while we were having dinner. My father would ask about our grades and if we were excelling in our studies. He would check our progress directly with the Headmaster. My brothers and I had to do well or we would be punished severely.

My mother had great respect and immense gratitude to George Ibrahim Abdallah, the Headmaster of the school at Bishmizene and, later on, Aba. She had always appreciated him for his determination and the sacrifices he made to educate the children of our district. I can understand why for I was a witness on an occasion when I was with my mother at home and Mr Abdallah visited with two of his instructors.

Mr Abdallah asked: 'Hanneh, where is Salim? You know the academic year is starting one week from now. How many of your children are you going to send to the school this year – two or three?'

My mother looked down and said in a soft voice, 'I really do not know. We are short of money and may have to send only one this year.'

He interrupted her, saying: 'Hanneh, who is asking you for money? Did I? You do not have to worry. Just send all your children to the school and I will teach them.'

My mother replied, 'Thank you very much. May God bless you. I shall tell Salim when he comes home, but we really cannot take advantage of your goodwill.'

From time to time, my mother would check on our conduct by talking with our teachers and classmates. For our part, we continually asked our parents: 'Can we have money to take with us to the school treasurer on account of our tuition?' The answer would be, 'Go and see the Headmaster and deliver this message – "Sir, respectfully we want to deliver a message from our father concerning payment of our tuition fees. He is not in a position to make a payment now and asks you to give us respite until he can sell the olive crop in season or sell a piece of property in the near future." '

This message usually worked, except one time when the Headmaster was desperate for money to pay overdue salaries to his teachers. Therefore, one Friday he announced during his 8.00 a.m. address to all students that, beginning the following Monday, the Director of Administration, Mr Fahd Ashalt, would not allow any student through the gate whose tuition was not paid in full.

Over the weekend we mentioned the issue of tuition to my father and stressed that we needed to take money with us to school on Monday, otherwise we would not be allowed to enter the premises. My father repeated the same statement that he did not have money at that time and the Headmaster would surely understand. My mother argued with my father, saying that he could not keep postponing the payment and he should provide the necessary funds. My father answered, 'I have no money now and the Headmaster will have to understand.' He also said, 'This is my business and you don't have to worry about it.'

My mother was not convinced but had to remain silent, keeping her worries to herself. On Monday we went to school as usual and, upon arrival, Mr Ashalt was at the gate and turned us away. With nothing else to do, we walked back home to Deddeh.

Arriving back home, my mother was furious with my father for not giving us the money, or at least part of it, to pay our tuition. That night, when my father came home from work my mother confronted him.

In response to my mother's tirade, my father asked us, 'Did you see the Headmaster and deliver my message?'

We answered, 'No, because we were not allowed inside the gate to talk to him.'

He said, 'All right. I'll go to see him at his village and ask him for this special favour. Your Headmaster is a friend of mine and surely he won't let me down.'

Hearing my father's statement, my mother shouted in a loud voice: 'How many times have you asked him for such favours over the past two years? Find the money, sell land, but please don't keep postponing the payment of school fees.'

My father simply said, 'Do you think it's easy to sell land? Please Hanneh, I know my duty and I shall go immediately and talk to the Headmaster.'

That evening my father, having been away for some time, returned to say that everything was in order and that in the morning we should report to school as usual.

Sure enough, the next day we encountered no problem at school and were allowed in. Before entering the classrooms, all the students were, as usual, assembled in the school playground to listen to the morning address by the Headmaster. To my surprise he said that he was sorry to learn that the Zakhem brothers had not been allowed into school the previous day due to the delay in payment of their tuition fees. The Headmaster mentioned that the measures taken the day before were directed at students whose families were perfectly capable of paying their fees but were failing to do so. Continuing on, the Headmaster mentioned the names of a few students who fell into this category. He then went on to say that the rule barring entry to children of delinquent families did not apply to those like the Zakhems, whose parents were making all kinds of sacrifices and were doing their best to keep up with the payment of tuition fees.

In June 1948 I obtained a Primary Certificate, which was a great achievement. My parents were very proud, for there were no more than ten children in our village – including my eldest brother Antoine – who had achieved the same qualification. The people in our village congratulated my parents on my success. I was pleased with myself, and my parents were determined to send me to a secondary school in Tripoli.

Going to Tripoli meant a major change in my lifestyle because I would have to move to the city and live as a student on half-board together with my eldest brother, Antoine, who was already enrolled there. My school Headmaster, George Ibrahim Abdallah, was very upset about my proposed move to Tripoli and he confronted my parents, saying 'Why don't you leave him at my school for his secondary education? You've already moved his brother and now you're moving George. It is unfair that after I train my students and provide them with an excellent education they should leave for another school that will reap the benefits of them being there. Please reconsider your decision.'

My parents replied firmly, but in a kind and considerate way: 'Mr George, we're very grateful for your help and we'll never forget what you've done for both our boys. We'll be forever indebted to you, but take into account that you still have two of our children, Abdallah and Najibah. After a great deal of thought and discussion we have decided that our son George, like Antoine, should follow an English programme. It's better for his future.' The Headmaster finally acknowledged the wisdom behind this decision and said, 'I care a lot for the Zakhem family and I'll not stand in your way.'

There is no doubt that Headmaster Abdallah sacrificed everything he owned to keep his school financially viable solely for the benefit of his students. In fact, it is no exaggeration to say that George Ibrahim Abdallah was instrumental in shaping the future of most of the young Lebanese from our district who graduated from Lebanese and foreign universities in the 1950s and 1960s. This class of graduates included men like the late Khalil Salem, General Secretary of the Treasury; Dr Elie Salem, President of Balamand University and a former Minister of Foreign Affairs; Ambassador Zafer Alhasan, former Secretary-General of the Ministry of Foreign Affairs; Dr Naim Atteyeh, a university Professor; and of course my brothers and myself. Nearly all of the children of the families in our district such as the Jeha, Moufarrej, Khouzami, Malek, Chammas, and Taleb were at George Ibrahim Abdallah's school. Headmaster

Abdallah exerted great efforts to educate as many sons of Al Koura district as he possibly could.

He was endowed with that great spirit of service to the community that characterises many successful Lebanese urban dwellers. He had a charismatic personality and a big heart. His love for education, especially the education of the children in the thirty-eight villages of Al Koura district was phenomenal. During the Second World War when money was scarce and schools practically did not exist, he opened his own private school and travelled to all the villages in the district visiting all the families there to encourage them to send their children to school. Many of us, including my own brothers and sisters, and myself, would not have been able to receive an education if George Ibrahim Abdallah had not established a school in our district. To him, lack of money was never an impediment. He decided to sell some of his properties to pay for the high expenses for the maintenance and operation of the school. Next to my parents, he was the first person who impressed upon me that in life one has to give and sacrifice for the sake of others. I will never forget how he used to receive us at the school door with open arms and a big smile. Tragically, he died in an accident involving the school bus at the young age of thirty-seven. He died because he gave his seat, which was next to the driver, to another instructor while he stood on the steps outside the door. A year earlier he had married a fine lady who, at the time of his death, was carrying his child. Three months later, she gave birth to a son. The entire district was shaken by the news of George Ibrahim Abdallah's tragic death, and every family felt the loss as though he were one of their own children. Everyone wondered what would happen now to the education of their children. Before long, a few schools were opened, however, only those who could pay the full tuition fees could register. I remember well how many parents at the time could not afford the tuition fees to send their children to school. George Ibrahim Abdallah's memory is still indelibly etched in my heart and in the heart of many others who were the recipients of his bounties. His love for education and the personal sacrifices he made to help many of his students, especially those who were talented and promising, will never be forgotten.

*   *   *

Men Who Dream, Can Do

In October 1948, I enrolled in Tripoli College High School which was founded by Ilias Milhim and located on the edge of the city in a newly developed area. Mr Milhim himself spent all his working life as a teacher at Tripoli Boys High School, known as TBS, a branch of the International College in Beirut. Upon retirement, he felt there was a need for another high school to follow the American programme of education, so he started a new institution. With his experience in administration and management, Tripoli College quickly gained a good reputation and attracted a sizeable number of students comparable to that of TBS.

Once again my father, being the shrewd man that he was, enrolled us at Tripoli College because he could negotiate better terms for payment of our tuition. This was so because Mr Milhim was a native of Kafarhazir, a village in our district. He was also a friend of our family and understood the financial limitations of my parents.

I was enrolled as a half-board student at Tripoli College. There I joined my brother Antoine who was already two years ahead of me. I was properly briefed and guided on how to adapt to this change in my life. It was a new school and a totally different environment from the one at Aba. Tripoli, the capital of North Lebanon, was very crowded and noisy compared to the village life to which I was accustomed. Motorcars and horse-driven carts moved about the streets; people walked on sidewalks or sat in coffee houses and restaurants. Approximately ten cinema halls were located in the neighbourhood of our school, which was a complete novelty to me.

At school I came into contact with students from different parts of Lebanon such as Tripoli, Akkar, Al Batroun, and Al Koura. In addition, our school had a few students from Palestine, Syria, Iraq, and Jordan. Palestinian, Iraqi, and Jordanian students were different from us Lebanese because they were enrolled as full-board students and lived in separate dorms. Later on we learned that their respective governments paid all of their expenses. This arrangement suited Mr Milhim very well because it meant that their fees were paid in full at the beginning of the academic year without delay. My case, and that of my brother, was just the opposite and an alternative arrangement had to be made between my father and Mr Milhim. We paid 10 per cent of our total fees upon registration and the balance in instalments spread over the year. Because my father could not always raise enough money from his trading business to pay the instalments on time, he was always asking Mr Milhim to give him more time to resolve the problem. Mr Milhim, although deaf, was always able to understand my father's requests and gave him a sign that he understood. Mr Milhim had become adept at lip reading. Sometimes my father conversed with him for fifteen minutes as they stood across from each other in one of the streets or in Al Koura Square in the city.

I witnessed one such conversation as I was walking with my father on the sidewalk of Al Koura Square where my father was trying to buy me a pair of shoes. Suddenly, we were intercepted by Mr Milhim who looked my father straight in the eye and said in a loud voice: 'Salim, when will you pay me the balance of the tuition for your children? I need the L.L.200 now as I am going to do my shopping for the boarding students.'

My father looked at him totally puzzled and said: 'Mr Milhim, you have always been kind and patient with me, but I must beg your indulgence as I do not have the money now. I have been trying to collect what I am owed from my clients since 7:00 this morning but no one has paid me so far. I shall continue my efforts tomorrow.'

Mr Milhim insisted that my father should pay him immediately and said: 'Surely you must have some money in your pockets. Check and see.'

My father took out L.L.10 and said, 'This is all I have and I need it to buy my son a pair of shoes.'

Mr Milhim interrupted, saying: 'No. Give it to me. I can buy vegetables with it.'

My father gave him the money and told me that buying my shoes would have to be postponed for a day or two. It seemed to me that buying my shoes would depend on whether or not we met Mr Milhim again.

As a child I had some understanding of the problems my father faced in providing for his family, but I had only the vaguest inkling of the challenges my fellow Lebanese experienced as they struggled to master the upheavals associated with their newly acquired national independence. Lebanon, like all Arab countries, had to reform old institutions and create new ones, and these are not easy tasks even for a naturally industrious people. For Lebanon the situation was perhaps more complex than for other Arab countries because the Lebanese were determined to build a democratic system with competitive politics, free press, and an independent judiciary.

Moreover, all of this had to be done within the context of a multi-cultural, multi-religious society with long-standing tendencies of fractiousness.

At the same time, Lebanon's search for unity and national cohesion was also an opportunity. Despite their divisions and conflicts, the Lebanese have spent more time living in peace together than in fighting each other. The country remains a democracy to this very day – imperfect, of course, but still the closest thing the Arab world has to a democracy and, as such, this is a remarkable achievement. If the twenty-first century is to be peaceful, then the peoples of the world must learn lessons drawn from Lebanon's experiment in multi-religious coexistence. Lebanon has experienced its failings (and what country has not?), but these must not obscure Lebanon's successes and its ability to serve as an example, not only to other Arabs but also to all people.

Lebanon's complexity – especially its capacity for generating both cooperation and conflict – has long fascinated foreign observers. I recall how in 1979 I met Ronald Reagan, then the former Governor of California and aspirant to the US presidency. At that time, he had not yet secured the nomination of the Republican Party. This meeting was arranged by my good friend, Michel T. Halbouty, who is of Lebanese origin and was a very close friend of Ronald Reagan. Also present at this meeting was Richard Allen, who had briefly served in the Nixon White House and would soon become President Reagan's first National Security Advisor. At one point in our conversation, Reagan posed a question along the following lines: 'Who on earth can explain Lebanese politics to an outsider like me? Is there anybody who can actually shed light on what's going on in Lebanon?' At that time, of course, Lebanon was in the throes of a destructive civil war.

Reagan then shared with me his own analysis of the Lebanese situation: 'This war in your country,' he said, 'started as a conflict between opposing Lebanese factions that either supported or rejected the Palestinian presence in Lebanon. Eventually, it developed into a Christian-Muslim war. Finally, it has become a Christian-Christian war.' More than a quarter of a century later, this fault-line in the Christian community still prevails. Similarly, and what is even more dangerous now, is the fault-line in the Muslim community, between the Shiites and Sunnis, that did not exist before.

Recollections of my Childhood

I am neither a politician nor a political analyst, and so I claim no special insight for solutions to the perennial dilemma of forging a national Lebanese consensus. As I see matters, though, the fundamental problem is that no individual or group has been able to define the exact nature of the Lebanese state in a way that is acceptable to all major Lebanese factions. Since 1943 many prominent authors and thinkers have attempted to define a broadly accepted state but their efforts have failed. Today, Lebanon still awaits the architect of her destiny.

* * *

To return to my narrative, one of the greatest challenges Lebanon faced during the period of my childhood – and one that continues to reverberate to this day in Lebanon and the whole Middle East – was the issue of Palestine. During my first week at school in Tripoli, war broke out in Palestine between the Arab states and Israel. After the war started, trucks full of men roamed around the streets of the city calling on young men to join the Arab army to defend Palestine and its people. Campaigns were also launched to provide assistance to Palestinians who had fled their homes, left behind all their property, and were seeking refuge in neighbouring countries.

As a new state with relatively weak government institutions – lacking, in fact, proper armed forces beyond a small and poorly equipped constabulary – Lebanon was in no position to mount a military campaign against Israel in support of the Palestinians. In other ways, however, the Lebanese went all out to support their Arab brethren, most notably by looking after the welfare of large numbers of Palestinian refugees. In this regard, there is no doubt that Lebanon's contribution surpassed that of any other Arab country and, quite possibly, of all the other Arab countries combined.

Most of the Palestinians who came to Tripoli during this period had mastered the English language because their country had been under British rule and they had, therefore, studied in English-run schools. Their language skills gave them an advantage over most Lebanese who were French educated. Practically overnight, being able to speak English became important in the Tripoli region. The determination of my parents to have their children trained in English proved to be a wise decision.

Given their language skills, many of the Palestinians were

employed by the Iraq Petroleum Company (IPC), which had just started building an oil refinery. The oil was refined from a supply that was pumped via a pipeline that ran from Kirkuk, Iraq, to Tripoli, Lebanon. In fact, some Palestinian staff members were transferred by IPC from its Haifa refinery in Palestine to take positions at the Tripoli facility.

In the following years, IPC was a major player in the economy and also the social life of Tripoli. Shops and restaurants grew in number, a gambling casino with a nightclub was established, and cinemas playing American films began to appear in the city. The first Beach Club on Lebanon's Mediterranean shore where men and women could swim in a private environment was founded by IPC. A carefully designed system of transportation serving all IPC employees was also adopted.

Palestinians who had worked with IPC and who were a majority among its Arab staff lived a comfortable life. Each family had an apartment in the best area of Tripoli and most had their own private cars, a luxury previously known only to very few wealthy families.

Less privileged Palestinians without any means of livelihood lived in refugee camps located near the city. They lived on a monthly subsidy paid by UNRWA (United Nations Relief Work Aid). The UN agreed to assist Palestinian refugees while they were in Lebanon pending a settlement with Israel. More than half a century later, the Arab-Israeli conflict remains unresolved, and the Palestinians are still in Lebanon, now in much larger numbers. Generation after generation of Palestinians has been born knowing nothing other than living in a refugee camp.

The British staff of IPC had their own quarters specially built at Mont Michel – a location on a hill overlooking Tripoli City – and they formed their own community with a private club and hospital. To see British people as civilians and not in army uniform as we did during the last years of the war was a novelty. As a result, English gained in importance and most schools introduced it as a third or alternative second language after Arabic.

I spent three years at Tripoli College (1948–51), during which time I was thoroughly absorbed in my studies. I was living on the premises as a half-board student, meaning that I was provided sleeping quarters but no meals. Instead, my father delivered food to my brother and me on a daily basis. This meant we saw our father every day and he took the opportunity to pose inevitable questions: 'Are you doing well at school? Are you studying hard?' We always answered, 'Yes, father.'

During weekends we went back to our home village and ate well from our mother's home cooking. I could hardly afford to go to the cinema more than once a month, except on occasions when I was invited by one of my classmates, Salim Habib, whose family owned four cinemas in Tripoli. Salim was a nice fellow and a good friend. Because his family was wealthy, all the other students in the school envied him. His wealth was readily visible as he would arrive at school, always well dressed, in his family's chauffeur-driven car. Salim's parents enrolled him as a boarding student at school so that he could be disciplined to study and obtain good grades.

The usual break from school was to go once a month to the cinema with one or two friends. However, the most significant outing I remember was one that occurred a month before Easter when my father took my two brothers and me to the tailor shop in the heart of the city to be measured for new suits. After that we went to a nearby restaurant and had a nice meal. The owner of the tailor shop, Nouri, and the proprietor of the restaurant, Subhi, were friends of my father and complimented him for sending us to school and looking after us so well. We then returned to school and my father carried on shopping for us and other members of our family.

In order to gain entry to the American University of Beirut (AUB) it was necessary to receive good grades and graduate from high school with an excellent average. Tripoli College was authorised to recommend senior students with high grades and good character for admission to AUB. Fortunately, in June 1951, I was among six students from a graduating class of fifty-five to be so recommended. I was overjoyed and my parents were proud that their second son had graduated from high school and was going on to AUB, just like his elder brother. The Headmaster and the teachers of my high school congratulated my parents, and I remember how the people of our village joined in a special celebration to commemorate the occasion.

On Commencement Day, which was held in Cinema Roxy Hall in Tripoli, the graduation ceremony was attended by my parents and a few of our relatives. To this day I remember this milestone in my life.

CHAPTER 2

Parents

I have already recounted the story of how in 1912 my grandfather emigrated from Lebanon to Brazil. Like many other Lebanese of that era, he was fleeing his homeland, which was then under the brutal rule of the Ottoman Turks. Of the Lebanese who left Lebanon between 1860 and 1920, most emigrated to Brazil. Today, the number of Brazilians of Lebanese heritage is twice as large as the population of Lebanon itself. During the First World War of 1914 to 1918, when many Lebanese died of illness and starvation, my grandfather was profoundly touched by the tragic news of the circumstances in his homeland. He wanted very much to help in any way he could and was desperately worried about the family he had left behind, but he could do nothing due to lack of communication at that time. My grandfather died in 1918, leaving my grandmother to raise her children as a widow. She gained the respect and admiration of the people of her village for her loyalty and devotion to the memory of her husband and her loving care for her family.

My grandfather on my mother's side, Abdallah Zakhem, was the elected Mayor of the village for twenty-eight years. I remember his father Mikhael who passed away in the early 1940s at the age of a 105 with good health but weak eyesight. My grandfather was highly respected by the people of the village as he was always there ready to listen to their problems and to try and solve them. As Mayor, his responsibilities touched every family in the village. For example, he had to issue birth certificates and process identity cards for newborns. He also had to accompany police officers when someone in the village had to be arrested. Arrests were frequent during the Second World War as many people were prosecuted for political reasons. In addition, my grandfather was a 'master mason' by profession. The villagers would come to him to construct a new home or an extension to a house to accommodate a newly married son, for example. All houses were built of limestone which was quarried and cut to size by hand from neighbouring fields and transported on mules and donkeys to the working site.

In order to assist the Mayor in the general security of the village, another person was elected by the people as a Watchman. His duties were to look after the security and safety of houses and the properties that belonged to them from theft and trespassing. Hanna Tannous Al Kobrossi was elected for this job at various terms so he would report any findings on a daily basis to my grandfather. This created a close relationship between them.

Throughout his life, my father totally obeyed his uncle Suleiman who was the brother of his father. He emigrated to Brazil for a few years at the end of the nineteenth century and came back around 1908. He did not want to leave the village any more, satisfied with the property he owned which he had planted with olive trees and fruit trees of all kinds such as grapes, figs, almonds and some citrus trees. His brother Tannous left for Brazil after his return and died there. So my father with his brother and sister were brought up to consider him as a father, and my brothers and sisters and I considered him as a grandfather. Ever since we were children and until he passed away in the late 1970s we used to address him always as 'grandfather'. The people of the village entrusted him with the affairs of the church, and he and the priest shouldered this responsibility.

Every Sunday we would go to church with my parents and after the ceremony we would go with our father to the butcher shop to buy some meat for my mother to prepare the Sunday meal at home. Meat was only available on Sundays and we used to eat vegetables that were mostly home-grown all the other days. The main dish on Sunday was *kibbe nayyeh*, and to prepare this dish the red meat would be placed in a large marble stone and beaten hard by a heavy wooden hammer until it was ground, then mixed with wheat and herbs and served as a steak tartare dish. Every Sunday at midday the sound of banging the wooden hammer on the *jurun* to grind the meat was heard throughout the village. This forty-five-minute process was done by every housewife in every home, and it became common knowledge that when this sound was heard it meant it was Sunday. It was also customary to have *arak*, an alcoholic drink locally produced from grapes, with the meal.

Men Who Dream, Can Do

Just before the First World War, Hanna Yaccub Al-Zakhem, cousin of my grandfather Abdallah, came back to Lebanon from Argentina with a small fortune. As he was a master tailor, he set up his tailor shop in Tripoli city and built an impressive large house in the village. A few years later he married Matilda, a girl from Amioun, the largest village in Al Koura. My parents had great respect for him as he was knowledgeable and very well acquainted with politicians and senior civil servants. As a sign of respect, they used to address him as 'uncle Hanna'. They also consulted him on matters that related to the family. In fact 'uncle Hanna' was asked by my father to become our godfather and he did for the three of us: Antoine, Abdallah, and myself. He had seven sons and one daughter. I remember well from my childhood how the Deddeh volleyball team of six members was composed of five brothers from his family, and one only from another. In summer seasons they used to challenge teams of other villages in the district and always won these games. As a child I used to accompany the team on foot to attend the game. On our way back to the village, we would be chanting and clapping all the way in celebration.

I was always fascinated by the stories told by the elderly people in the village. My 'grandfather' Suleiman used to trace his stories back to the days when he was in Brazil. Another person in the village, Simon Saad, would trace his stories back to the days when he was in Detroit, US, working for the Ford Auto Factory. He used to boast that Henry Ford spoke to him while he was working on his bench. While in the US, Simon learned how to become a barber and when he returned to the village he would practise this profession. He carried his tools in a small briefcase and a foldable chair and would tour the village from house to house and pass through public places. If anyone needed a haircut, Simon would immediately unfold the chair, open the briefcase, and do the job. In the process, he recited his stories which were mostly the same unless a new one came to him from certain sources.

Here in London, I discovered another barber, David, who has been coming to my house or office to cut my hair for the past twenty-five years. David also cuts the hair of a few of my friends in our community and he tells you all the news in the twenty minutes he spends on the job. My mind, however, goes back to the days in my village Deddeh and the wealth of memories it entails.

Parents

One story I can never forget, as told by Hanna Kobrossi in a very dignified manner, was the story of how my father met and married my mother:

> One day your grandmother Tarfa, whom I respect and admire, said to me: 'Hanna, Salim needs to be married.' I said, 'I agree, Salim is now a young man and he really ought to get married. I believe Hanneh, the daughter of Abdallah Zakhem, the Mayor of the village, would suit him well.' Grandmother Tarfa said, 'It's a very good idea and I shall meet the Mayor and solicit his opinion on the subject and let you know.'
>
> The Mayor's answer to your grandmother's initial enquiry was encouraging, so one evening I arranged to visit the Mayor with your grandmother and formally propose on behalf of your father. During the visit Hanneh, your mother, served us coffee and I sat next to her father, the Mayor. I addressed the Mayor by saying, 'Abdallah, you now know why Tarfa and Salim are here, so let's waste no time. How about getting this orphan Salim married to this orphan Hanneh? Please give us your blessing. After all, Tarfa is from the same family and is well-known to you.'

Abdallah immediately gave his approval and consent and my mission was accomplished.

Hanna Tannous was very proud of his achievement, and he repeated this story to me and to my brothers and sisters on several occasions. He greatly admired my parents, who were able to raise a unique family in the village: a total of five boys and three girls, all of whom had received a good education.

My parents lived their lives with abundance in the village, Deddeh, and maintained good and friendly relations with everyone there. They also extended this friendship to people from other villages in the district of Al Koura. Al Koura is famous for its olive groves, the source of olive oil and green and black olives that we consume in our daily food. Even when we took a flat in Beirut in the neighbourhood of the AUB campus in 1959 to provide residence for my brothers and sisters who were studying at the university, my father refused to leave the village and would only make weekend visits to Beirut. My mother divided her time between the two.

My parents were simple, loving people. They loved people, and people loved them in return. Of the many friends they had, Adib

Salem, from the neighbouring village of Bterram was the closest. Adib was the Notary Public of Al Koura district, and an official intermediary between its citizens and the government. Adib was also a councillor and informal Justice of the Peace for the district. My grandfather and Adib were very good friends and they exchanged visits frequently. Adib and my father also knew each other well, and Adib always reminded my father that he was a most fortunate man to have married my mother. They both liked big families; each sired eight children, and each was committed to giving his children the highest education possible. This was the major dream shared by both Adib's family and my parents: the education of their respective children. While education was important to the families in Al Koura, to the Salems and the Zakhems it was an obsession – an overriding commitment. How, with very limited means, they could have such high hopes, I do not know. The fact that they realised their objective is nothing short of miraculous. Not only were my father and Adib good friends, but we, as their children, continued this friendship. Whenever we meet, we recall with deep admiration the sacrifices made by our parents for our sake. It is my hope that these affectionate ties between the two families continue to thrive.

My father was heavily engrossed in trading the two main products of the village: olive oil and lime. But he was always on the lookout to buy land with olive groves. He also wanted to have an olive oil press, which would give him a certain prestige in the community. Having a press meant that he could control the process of oil extraction from its seed not only from our crop but for others in the village. He could also produce one or two products with an olive oil base such as soap. His wish was realised in 1963 when my brother Abdallah started working with me and we were able to allocate the funds to buy the press. My father believed in land ownership and always had a plan for us to invest any surplus money in land acquisition.

As I mentioned earlier, a great concern for my parents was the education of their children. They were willing to go to great lengths and do whatever they could to achieve it. However, there was a major financial problem and to resolve it they had no alternative but to sell the land they had both inherited from their parents. On certain occasions this was not possible because no one was interested in buying land. Therefore, my father had to resort to borrowing money from private lenders at a very high interest rate. In 1960, when three of my brothers and sisters were at AUB and I was the only one helping him financially from the money I earned, my father was desperate for help. He knew from my brother Abdallah, who was in his third year in the Engineering School, that he had applied to obtain a Point IV Scholarship (a US government scholarship awarded to three deserving Lebanese students at AUB), and that a decision would be taken by the end of September before student enrolment in October. The committee that would decide was made up of three members: a representative of the Ministry of Education, another one on behalf of the Point IV Scholarship, and finally the Dean of Engineering.

Their decision did not include my brother Abdallah, although his grades were higher than the three recipients. My father was very annoyed and in a moment of despair he decided to visit the Dean of the Engineering School and plead his case. Abdallah would not allow him to do so, and my father kept quiet about it. At 7:00 the following morning, he walked to the main gate of AUB where he met the gatekeeper Abu Aziz. They knew each other very well as my father used to bring Abu Aziz a present of four gallons of olive oil from our crop in Deddeh ever year. He asked Abu Aziz how he could meet the Dean of Engineering. Abu Aziz replied, 'He is very important and I don't know if he will accept to meet with you.' 'Don't worry about that,' my father said. 'Just tell me how to reach his office.'

Abu Aziz instructed my father accordingly and my father went directly to the office of the Dean and said, 'I want to see the Dean.'

The receptionist promptly replied, 'Who are you and do you have an appointment?'

'No, I don't,' my father said, 'but I need to see him.'

The receptionist told my father that the Dean would not be in the office before 8:30 a.m., and that he should go and talk to the secretary of the Dean. My father went to the secretary's office and repeated his request. The secretary was adamant that she could not and would not allow him to see the Dean without a prior appointment.

My father was also adamant in saying, 'It is up to you, but I shall wait for him here until he comes.'

At around 8:30 a.m. Dean Weidner walked in, looked over his shoulder at my father, and went straight to his office followed by his secretary. She told him that my father was the father of Abdallah Zakhem, a third year engineering student, and that he was waiting to be seen. A few minutes later my father was called into the Dean's office. He walked in, sat down, looked towards the secretary and said, 'I want you to please translate what I say to him, word for word.'

He then turned around to face the Dean and said: 'I am the father of Abdallah Zakhem. I have two other children studying at the university and I am not capable of paying for their expenses. I need help.'

The Dean reviewed Abdallah's file while listening to my father.

My father continued: 'My son is one of the first in his class. Last year he applied for a Point IV Scholarship but was not selected, and the same thing has happened this year. The committee selected three students who are financially secure and whose parents are rich. I understand that America is here to fight communism, but is this the way to do it? By helping the rich and neglecting the deserving poor? That is all I have to say. I hope I have made myself understood.'

Two days later, Abdallah was awarded a Point IV Scholarship to cover his tuition, plus $30 monthly pocket money. My father saw this as a great achievement, and so did I.

In 1981, during the Christmas holidays, we celebrated the golden wedding anniversary of my parents in Nairobi, Kenya. All my brothers and sisters attended along with their families. My youngest brother, Albert, however, was still a bachelor at that time. Our business was growing well on all fronts; in fact, faster than we had expected. It occurred to me to ask my father if he had any special wish or desire to fulfil.

I said to him: 'You are well into your seventies. You've raised us to become what we are today. Is there any wish you aspire to fulfil at this stage of your life?'

He answered without hesitation saying, 'Yes. I want to go to Brazil and visit my father's grave and learn more about his life there. I want to find out where he is buried and try to move his remains to the village of Deddeh.'

'Father,' I replied, 'do you know if any of his friends are still alive who can guide you in this search?'

'Yes, I know Siman Haider and the Bishop of our Greek Orthodox Church of Antioch. Just before his departure for Brazil to take up his ecclesiastical post there, the Bishop promised to help me.'

Without any hesitation I promised my father that I would arrange for someone who speaks English and Arabic to accompany him on his trip to Brazil.

A few weeks after I had this conversation with my father, I visited the United States. It was there that I met Asaad Najjar, a family friend and business partner who was then living in Arlington, Texas. He had fled with his family to escape the Lebanese civil war. Asaad was six years younger than my father. In the course of speaking with him about our business partnership in real estate and the war in Lebanon, I mentioned that my father wanted to visit Brazil hoping to learn more about his father's life there and to visit his grave. Realising that my father needed someone to travel with him, Asaad did not hesitate to volunteer to go with him, saying he had relatives and friends in Brazil who would look after my father. I was very pleased and grateful that Asaad had offered to travel with my father to Brazil. I immediately made the necessary travel arrangements to Rio de Janeiro for both of them.

My father travelled to Houston, and from there went with Asaad to Brazil. In Rio de Janeiro they met with the Bishop and other Lebanese immigrants who knew my grandfather. Fortunately, my father met Jacob Daniel, who is my age and is also from our home village of Deddeh. Jacob had emigrated to Brazil in the 1950s, and he very kindly acted as my father's local guide. Together they toured the cemeteries of Rio de Janeiro in which foreigners are buried. In one cemetery registry, they found a certificate that had no name filled in but did include a photograph that resembled my grandfather. The date of the document was correct, and local people who had known my grandfather ascertained that the picture was of him. My father, who had never met his father, was convinced that his search had been successful.

Upon returning to Deddeh, my father had a special mass in memory of my grandfather. After the mass, my father went to visit the grave of his mother and sprinkled a handful of earth he had taken from the grave of his father in Brazil. For seventy-three years my father had to suffer the experience of war and the demanding hardships of life, and throughout those years he never ceased to think about his father whom he had never seen. The memory of his father always moved him to tears. His trip to Brazil in search of his father's resting place was a great comfort to him, and I was so gratified that I had the privilege of helping my father fulfil his dream to visit Brazil and trace his father's footsteps. My father passed away in November 2003 at the age of ninety-five and my mother passed away in May 2006 at the age of ninety. Towards the end of his life there was a serenity about him that brought much comfort to those who were experiencing the turbulence of the time and the severe exigencies of life.

CHAPTER 3

The University Years

It was the first Monday of October in 1951, when I went to Beirut with my brother Antoine and my father to register as a freshman student at the American University of Beirut (AUB).

I consider myself very fortunate to have gained admission to AUB because it is the most prestigious university in the Middle East; ever since its foundation in 1866, it has offered an American system of liberal education. Second to AUB is Saint Joseph University (Université Saint-Joseph) which follows the French educational system. At that time, the Lebanese government was in the process of founding its own national institution of higher learning, which today is thriving as the Lebanese University.

During my time at AUB, the student body numbered around 1,500, distributed among four schools: Arts and Sciences, Engineering and Architecture, Agriculture, and Medicine. The standard of education offered at AUB was, and still is, comparable to the standard at the top ten to fifteen universities in the United States. Today, as was the case when I entered AUB, no student was accepted without a good recommendation. In addition to the recommendation, every student had to pass the demanding university entrance exam. In attending AUB I had an added advantage: my older brother, Antoine, began attending the university two years before me, so he was able to provide me with advice and guidance before, during, and after my enrolment.

This was only my second visit to Beirut, the capital city of my country. My first visit was in 1948 when students of our class at Aba school went to visit the regional headquarters of UNESCO (United Nations Educational, Scientific, and Cultural Organisation). Throughout its long history, which dates back some 6,000 years, Beirut has been a melting pot of civilisations. Enriched by a wealth of culture, a diverse society, and an advantageous geographical location, Beirut was an obvious choice for a UNESCO regional office. Lebanon, after all, was among the forty-seven founding members of the UN. A distinguished Lebanese diplomat, Dr Charles Malik, represented his country at the UN and served as a member of the UN Human Rights Commission. He also served in a pivotal role as the Commission's Rapporteur and later as its Chairman.

With this awareness of Beirut's cultural heritage, I presented myself at the Registrar's office of AUB where I was handed the necessary registration documents. The first requirement on the list was to obtain a medical report from the university doctor, so I went directly to the infirmary and had a complete physical check-up.

After seeing the doctor, I was taken on a guided tour of the campus. At that time, AUB was spread over an area of about fifty-two acres from the hilltop at Ras Beirut to the shore of the blue Mediterranean. Several AUB buildings offered a beautiful and unparalleled view of Beirut City. On the southern side of campus, along the campus boundary wall and the main gate, is Bliss Street, named after AUB President Dr Daniel Bliss. Various shops and restaurants line one side of this street, the most famous of which are the Faisal and Uncle Sam restaurants. Restaurant Faisal was the most reputable for quality of food, but it was also the most expensive. Although some professors were privileged to eat there, very few students could afford it and preferred to eat in the university cafeteria or other restaurants that were cheaper.

Restaurant Faisal was also renowned as a meeting place for the educated elite of the Arab world. It is worth mentioning that after fifty years in business, Faisal closed its doors in 1984, at the height of the civil war, when it became impossible to run. In 1990 it reopened under different ownership as a Pizza Hut – a total change from what it once was.

On my first day of registration I felt truly privileged to be a student at AUB. The US government recognised the university as being the best American university abroad, and students from all over the Middle East and Africa went there for an education that usually surpassed what could be obtained in their home country. In my freshman class, for example, I met Ethiopian, Sudanese, Bahraini, Syrian, and Iraqi students, in addition to Lebanese and Palestinian. Most of the non-Lebanese students were supported by their governments, which gave them tuition, board, and pocket money. Palestinian students, however, were fully sponsored by the

The University Years

UNRWA. For their part, Lebanese students had to rely on their parents for this kind of support. Naturally, my family bore a great burden in this respect.

Due to his limited income, my father did not have the necessary funds to pay our tuition. As the date of payment approached, my mother asked my father if he had arranged the money for the payment. He would always reply, 'With God's help, I'll manage.' But my mother urged him to give her proof that he had, otherwise she wanted him to sell some of the property she had inherited from her parents and use the proceeds to pay the tuition. Again, my father replied that he would manage.

'D' Day for registration and tuition payment was the first Monday in October. On that date, we took a car from Deddeh to Beirut to register at AUB. That morning, we woke up early so that we could stop in Tripoli before going on to Beirut. Our Tripoli visit was for the purpose of collecting money from an industrialist named Ibrahim Najjar. My father and Mr Najjar did business together in the olive oil trade. My father used to supply Mr Najjar's factory with the residue of the olive that is a by-product of the process of extracting oil from olives that is used in our daily food. Between mid-September and early October my father would have supplied a certain quantity of this product. According to him, the cost of this would cover our tuition payment and if not, he could still take advance money on future supplies. Although he received us with a big smile and commended my father for sending us to the university, Mr Najjar would not agree to pay my father more than what he was entitled to at that date. After much haggling in front of us, Mr Najjar told my father he would not accept his proposal to pay L.L.1,000, but would agree to pay L.L.400. Having no other choice, my father took the money and passed it to us saying that each of us would take L.L.200 to pay against our tuition and convince the Comptroller to accept the payment of the balance of L.L.600 in monthly instalments from then until the end of December.

* * *

On my second day at AUB, I continued registration procedures. In the registration building at West Hall, approximately fifteen university staff were sitting behind a long counter performing their duties. Each administrator looked at my registration paper, wrote something on it, slid it back inside my handbook, and then passed it to the next person (the handbook is a university identity card that must be carried by every student at all times). This went on until I reached the last member of the registration team, who was the Comptroller.

The Comptroller looked at me and said, 'George Zakhem, you need to pay L.L.600 as fees for the first semester. Please give me the money.'

My answer was that I had L.L.200 that I could pay and that the balance would be given in monthly instalments.

His reply was abrupt: 'Did you make arrangements with the Chief Comptroller?'

I answered, 'No, sir.' 'Then please,' he said, 'go and see him and come back to me.'

The office of the Chief Comptroller was located in another room and I had to make an appointment to see him like other students. However, these students had obtained scholarships from their governments or foundations like UNRWA and had only to verify this status with the Comptroller. My position was totally different as I had to prove that I could pay the balance by instalments, a good reason for him to keep me waiting to the last day before he finally agreed to see me. After a lengthy explanation I eventually obtained his agreement for delayed payment and went back to the Comptroller, paid L.L.200, completed the registration, and obtained my university handbook. From that moment on I felt like a king. I had been accepted as an undergraduate at AUB.

Freshman year was the most difficult academic year in the whole period I spent at AUB. I had to orient myself to cope with my new environment. My class had around 120 students, divided into five sections arranged systematically in alphabetical order. We took five courses per semester. After classes ended for the day, we had to go to the main library to do our homework for the following day. Each student was left to work on his own and if he needed any help he had to ask for a special appointment with his designated advisor. It was a totally different system from what I was accustomed to at our high school in Tripoli.

As freshman students, we were forced to stay on campus and we were not allowed to be outside campus after 7:00 p.m. except on Saturdays when the curfew was extended until 9:00 p.m. Our main source of entertainment, therefore, was to attend a movie at one of the new cinema houses at Canon Square Al Bourg in the commercial centre of Beirut. This meant we had to travel for about fifteen minutes by the tramway which cost 5 piaster (L.L.1 is equal to 100 piaster) each way. The entry ticket to the cinema cost 60 piaster and another 25 piaster for a falafel sandwich from the famous Freiha take-away shop, bringing the total to 95 piaster.

We used to look forward to this outing on Saturdays and we were in the habit of saving our money during the week to cover the expenses of our weekend outing. But at times, we decided to spend a bit more on ourselves and take refreshment like Coca-Cola, which cost 15 piaster. This meant that there was no money left for our fare on the tram. In such cases, we would play funny and innocent tricks. For example, we would board one end of the tram when the money collector was at the opposite end. As he turned to come our way, we would go the opposite direction, meeting each other halfway. When one of the collectors would discover our plan, he would stop us, shouting: 'Boys, please pay the fare!' In addition to Arabic, he would repeat it in English, French, and Armenian. Our answer was always the same: 'Sir, we are getting down at the next stop.' If he was not accommodating, we would jump from the tram as it was still moving, but most of the time we were allowed to stay. We would repeat this trick on the next tram until we arrived at the main gate of the university.

* * *

Being students from different schools and different backgrounds and nationalities, it was not easy to communicate with others or to make friends. In addition, my constant worry was how I could assist my father by obtaining a special scholarship or by getting part-time work to help pay for my tuition and upkeep.

Slowly I became acclimatised to the AUB environment and soon I was introduced to the Dean of Students, Mr Battey, who sympathised with me and helped me obtain part-time jobs on campus. During my years on campus I worked as a cashier in the main cafeteria and in the bookstore. I also did other occasional jobs like selling refreshments on Field Days and at folk dance festivals.

Dean Battey also organised a Student Co-operative Society for needy students that provided us with affordable accommodation on campus. For example, I lived with eleven other students in one room with six bunk beds. We operated a small laundry service for other students at a lower fee than the prevailing rate. We also established our own restaurant in the basement of West Hall for which each of us took responsibility for its operation on a weekly basis. The student in charge for the week acted as cook, waiter, and cashier. I recall an incident when a Chinese student was in charge of the restaurant. The first day of the week he cooked spaghetti with meatballs; the second day it was spaghetti with white sauce; and the third day gratin in the oven. We were annoyed and questioned him about having the same meal every day, especially because this meal was our one and only real meal for the entire day. He looked at us and said, 'Listen, what you said is not correct. What you had yesterday was spaghetti and what you are having today is macaroni, and if you do not like it you do the cooking!'

AUB's newly established Engineering School was due to receive its first class of students in October 1952. It was located in an impressive building donated to the university by the Bechtel Engineering Corporation and named after it. The timing was right for me to join as a first-year student because I completed my freshman year in the summer of 1952. The Dean of the school had been appointed the previous year. He was a former Marine Engineer and a Senior Officer in the United States Navy. AUB's President, Dr Stephen B. L. Penrose, Jr., had personally selected C. Ken Weidner for the post following an extensive search that lasted over a year. Dean Weidner's contribution to the establishment and development of the school was immense, and it became the most prestigious Engineering School in the Middle East.

Through Dean Weidner's connections with large US corporations and government institutions, he was able to secure the funds needed to furnish the school laboratories and workshops with the latest equipment and machinery. He also obtained long-term funding from private and public sources such as the Ford Foundation, USAID (Point IV), and UNRWA to assist students in need of scholarships. Emile Bustani joined the club of donors in offering CAT (Contracting and Trading Company) Loan-in-Aid funds to needy students. Academically, Dean Weidner created four different departments: Civil, Mechanical, Electrical, and Architecture. Over the years, Architecture gained more prominence and the school was renamed the School of Engineering and Architecture. These eventually became two separate schools: the School of Engineering, and the School of Architecture. A number of exceptionally competent professors were recruited from the United States, Britain, and Lebanon to join the faculty.

To qualify for a Bachelor of Engineering degree in any of the four disciplines, a student had to spend four academic years and three summers (five years total) in residence. Students were required to spend two summers off-campus in a special camp located in a remote area of Lebanon and one summer on an actual job site. This programme was designed to provide students with experience in the real world of field operations. As a result of these strenuous requirements, AUB graduates were considered to be highly skilled engineers.

Dean Weidner was devoted to the idea of creating an Engineering School that would serve the ambitious construction and development projects of countries located in the Middle East and Africa. He often said that his goal was not educating engineers who specialised in one field like civil or electrical, but he wanted to produce all-round development engineers who could make critical decisions even when working on projects in the middle of nowhere. For this reason, he said it was essential for AUB graduates to have a basic knowledge of all areas of engineering. Therefore, engineering students followed the same curriculum of studies for two and a half years and only after that, did they concentrate on a speciality.

In June 1953, I completed my first year and began a five-week, off-campus field surveying programme. Along with other students, I was billeted in a special camp located on the grounds of the Grand Hotel in Bhamdoun Village, which is close to Bhamdoun Town, a famous summer resort some 30 kilometres from Beirut on the road to Damascus. We occupied tents that each accommodated six students while instructors were accommodated in one special tent. Food in the camp was prepared and served from the hotel kitchen. Toilets and showers were built from concrete blocks to shoulder height without a roof. Only cold water was provided and we had to take showers on a daily basis.

Every week four students were put in charge of cleanliness and hygiene, including responsibility for toilets and showers. Some students felt that this work was below their dignity, but our senior instructor, who was Camp Manager, insisted good engineers had to experience doing such jobs. 'Imagine,' he would say, 'that as a future engineer you are called by the city to inspect a leak in a sewer and the only way to verify it is to go inside and inspect it visually. What will you do? Without doubt you will have to do it, so you must be prepared.' That ended the argument and there were no further complaints.

We students thoroughly enjoyed our five weeks in the camp, so much so that we would have liked to stay for the entire summer. But we had to leave to make way for the next group of students whose turn had come to receive camp training.

Our second summer term was spent in the Engineering School's mechanical shop on the AUB campus. The third summer term was spent off-campus on an actual job site. All students had to find a job with a private engineering company. Along with three other classmates (Fuad Abu Annasr, Emile Jeha, and Khairallah Lubbos), I took a job with CAT as a Trainee Engineer in Doha, Qatar, starting on July 1st 1955. Our salary was L.L.200 per month. To get to Doha, I had to take my first flight on an aeroplane, and I remember how we boarded the DC4 at Beirut airport. We flew to Basra for an overnight stay then took off the following morning for Doha, where we landed after three hours on a very primitive and rugged runway made out of consolidated sand sprayed with crude oil.

Summer in Qatar was akin to hell on earth. The temperature varied between 32°C and 47°C with relative humidity approaching 100 per cent. Air-conditioning did not exist and the ceiling fans that were installed in our living quarters provided only meagre relief. These quarters were temporary constructions built in the form of colonial army camps with various barracks of different sizes to accommodate between two and ten people each. Engineers were housed two per room, foremen and monthly-paid employees were housed three to four per room, and artisans eight to ten per larger sized unit. The mess hall was located in the centre of the camp and an administration office was adjacent to it for the Camp Manager. A large warehouse stood at one corner of the camp, and a workshop for motor vehicles and construction equipment was close by. Approximately 200 people lived in the camp at Ras Abuabboud, most of them from Lebanon but also some from Palestine, Syria, and Jordan.

The University Years

I was appointed to work as a Trainee Engineer at the Doha water supply project. This facility included a desalination plant and water distribution system. The Project Manager was Moufid Dabaghi, who had graduated from AUB in 1953. He was very capable and I learned a great deal from working with him. We also became friends and our friendship has lasted through the years to this very day. Moufid is a very refined and kind gentleman. Under his guidance, I gained considerable experience not only of construction issues but also of matters like overall working conditions that, strictly speaking, were outside our purview.

At 6:30 a.m. we boarded trucks and pick-ups which transported us to our different job sites in Doha. We returned to the camp at 12:30 p.m. to have lunch and rest from the heat until 3:00 p.m., when we went back to work until 6:00 p.m. We worked six days a week, Saturday through Thursday, nine hours per day, with Friday off. We ended each workday totally exhausted from the heat. The morning temperature was approximately 30°C and would rise to 47°C at midday and dip to around 36°C in the evening. The temperature of the sea water was over 30°C during the day, so it was not possible to take a swim before midnight.

One week after our arrival at Doha, most of us began to suffer from heat blisters and we required medical treatment. Due to excessive perspiration, we were instructed to take two salt tablets a day. Except for the excitement of doing something practical on a job site in support of our education, life was far from fun; in fact, it was difficult and harsh. Yet, looking back now, it was a worthwhile experience.

Although we had a contract to work for three months, at the end of the second month four of us decided to ask the Resident Engineer responsible for the company site to relieve us of our duties and allow us to return to Beirut. He was a reasonable person and gave us permission to leave after two weeks had elapsed. I left Doha accompanied by Emile Jeha on a DC4 flight that was chartered by the company. The aeroplane made regular cargo runs but was not equipped to carry passengers, and so it did not have air-conditioning or heating. For this reason, inside the aeroplane it was stifling hot when on the ground; and freezing cold when in the air. Emile and I were the only passengers on board, and we were given blankets and instructed to lie down on the floor of the aeroplane's cargo bay. Six hours later, we landed in Beirut and I went straight to my village, Deddeh. It was wonderful to be home and I had a great deal to tell my family. It was the middle of September and just two weeks before the new academic year began.

This was supposed to be my senior, and final, year at the AUB Engineering School. My brother Antoine was in his fourth year of Medical School. Another member of my family, my brother Abdallah, was to join us at AUB. All my father could contribute towards our tuition fees was L.L.400 supplemented by the L.L.300 I had earned working in Qatar. With this sum of money in hand, it would be difficult to register as a full-time student, so I decided to divide the remaining credit hours I needed to graduate into two semesters and take a part-time job. I registered for two courses, or eight credit hours, for the first semester and took a job with an engineer named Robert Najjar, who was a distributor of Trane air-conditioning units. I earned L.L.100 per month.

After holding this part-time job, I discovered after two months that I could not save any money out of my salary and, therefore, could not assist my family in paying any of my tuition. After consulting with my brother Antoine and my parents, I took the decision to suspend my studies after I finished the semester and return to work for CAT at one of their desert work sites. In doing so, I hoped that I would be able to save enough money to fund my final year at AUB.

I reported to the CAT office at Saifi in February 1956, where I met the Chief Engineer, Nicola Halaby. He offered me a job in Kuwait with a salary of L.L.400 per month for a period of six months. I was quite satisfied with the offer and travelled to Kuwait in March where I was posted as a Trainee Engineer on a water reservoir project at Shuwaikh. Living accommodation was similar to that in Qatar, but the facilities were more organised. The camp was located at Hawali, around five kilometres from Kuwait City centre and seven kilometres from the work site. The company provided buses to transport their employees between the camp and the project.

Climate conditions were more acceptable in March and April, but they deteriorated rapidly between May and August. Kuwait never really impressed me as a city, and I anxiously looked forward

The University Years

to the completion of my contract so I could return to my studies in Beirut. A few days before my departure the Project Manager, Farouk Shehabi, called me into his office and said, 'There is one person who would like to meet you to offer you something. Would you be interested in speaking with him?'

I agreed. The person in question then walked in and said, 'I am Suheil Farah, working as a contractor on highways and roads mainly for CAT. It has come to my knowledge that you are here to save some money and go back to school for one year to get your degree. I am a Lebanese from Almunsef and I am always prepared to help anyone in need when I can see they are doing their utmost to try and help themselves. Would you allow me to help you? Just tell me how much you need.'

I thanked him and said, 'I have made enough money to pay my tuition, but I still need some more to help my brothers.'

He said, 'That is fine with me. Please tell me how much you need and do not feel in the slightest way embarrassed because I shall expect you to repay the amount when you start earning money and are able to pay.'

After some thought, I thanked him and said that I would appreciate a loan of L.L.400. He immediately wrote me a cheque for the amount drawn on a Lebanese bank. I wrote him a promissory note and thanked him for his generosity. I repaid this loan four years later when we met again at the CAT offices in Beirut.

On my return trip to Beirut in September 1956, I stopped in Baghdad for ten days. Salman Asafwani's family served as my host. Salman was the owner and Chief Editor of one of the leading Arabic daily newspapers in Iraq, *Al-Yaqza*. He was married to Ramza, a relative of my family from Bishmizene. They met in Baghdad when Ramza was visiting her sister, Foutine, who worked as a couturier to the royal family. Her youngest sister, Hanan, worked with her in Baghdad while their eldest sister, Mouhaba, stayed in Bishmizene where she married Taleb Barakat. Foutine was my godmother and the godmother of all my brothers and sisters as well.

Salman's eldest son, Ramiz, was my age and attended the American University of Beirut from 1954 to 1956, and so he and I were contemporaries at AUB. We had become good friends, and it was upon his insistence that I made this visit to Baghdad. I was highly impressed by the city and its people, to the extent that I felt that Baghdad was more advanced than Beirut. The streets were large and clean, with traffic lights and well-displayed signs. Public transportation included double-decker buses, and there were regular bus stops clearly marked on street sidewalks. A few homes also had televisions.

Iraqi Airways introduced turbo jet Viscount aeroplanes on their routes far ahead of any other airline in the Middle East, although in fairness Middle East Airlines was the second in line to follow suit. I also learned that the Iraqi government provided social security and medical care for its people. Free education at all levels was also available, and a great number of deserving students were sent for higher and specialised education at universities abroad, mostly to Western countries. Life in Baghdad seemed to me to be well organised. At the end of this most enjoyable holiday, I flew to Beirut on the Iraqi Airways Viscount service hoping that my first job after graduating from AUB would be in Iraq.

I spent around two weeks with my parents and family in our village of Deddeh. During the first week of October, my brothers Antoine and Abdallah and I reported to the Registrar's office, where we went through the registration process without any problems. The three of us were each in our senior year: Abdallah to graduate from Section Secondaire with *Baccalaureate Deuxième Partie*; myself with a degree in Mechanical Engineering; and Antoine with a Doctoral degree in Medicine.

As I went through the registration process for the last time, I discovered that I was short by L.L.160, which I needed to buy textbooks. Without hesitation I decided to ask the head of the Department of Engineering, Professor Walter Baggaley, for help. I made an appointment and went to see him, explained my problem, and requested a special loan from the school to be paid back during the first year after my graduation.

Without any hesitation Professor Baggaley took a cheque book from his drawer, wrote a personal cheque for L.L.200, and said: 'Take this, my son, and purchase the books you need.'

I thanked him and said, 'I am so grateful for your generosity. Please let me write you an IOU saying I promise to return this money two months after I graduate.'

He interrupted me: 'George, I do not want this money from you.

Remember there is always someone who is in desperate need of help; just remember this when in the future you come across someone who is in legitimate need of help and you are in a position to do something about it. It will be this that will give me the greatest satisfaction.'

On reporting the story to my parents, they were also very grateful and showered the professor with their blessings and good wishes.

My final year at the School of Engineering went relatively smoothly. In fact, at long last I found time to participate in school sports and social programmes. I joined the volleyball team, and that year we won minor and major league championships. Dean Weidner was a great believer in sport, encouraging students to participate in all kinds of sporting activities.

It was customary for the Department of Physical Culture at AUB to train students in track and field events, which were individual sports. The department did not, however, promote team games such as football, volleyball, or basketball. But Dean Weidner believed that a spirit of teamwork was essential to good engineering, and so he encouraged his students to participate actively in team sports. He would always support the teams by attending major games, especially those held between the School of Engineering and the School of Arts and Sciences. Dean Weidner's efforts paid off when, under his leadership, our school won most of the major league championships at AUB for nine consecutive years.

Social activities were carried out with the same vigorous spirit. Two main functions topped the list of events held by the Engineering Student Society (ESS) during the academic year: the Engineering Show, and the Engineering Ball. Both functions were held at the West Hall Auditorium and Ballroom. I participated as an actor in more than two ESS shows and in every ESS ball. Both functions were highly rated by all AUB students. Fierce competition existed between the Medical Student Society, the Arts and Sciences Student Society, and the Engineering Student Society. We engineers always came in first and received tremendous encouragement from the students, faculty, and staff of our school. The student weekly paper, *Outlook*, published articles in which ESS's productions were highly rated.

Other functions, such as the Saturday evening dance parties, were also held at the Engineering building. Since all the students at the school were male, we invited girls from the Beirut College for Women, which originally was founded as a Junior College. They were always pleased to attend and we all had a great time. We also organised day outings to various places of interest in Lebanon. On Saturday, April 1st 1955, the *Outlook* weekly paper carried a front page story describing how an earthquake had hit the Engineering building and destroyed it. The story said that Dean Weidner, some faculty, and students had been injured. Those of us in the Engineering School were surprised by this story because we had been taking our Saturday quizzes at the time the earthquake was reported.

Upon investigation we discovered that the writer, who was an Arts and Sciences student, had played an 'April Fool's' joke. Obviously, this did not go down well with us engineering students, and so we took immediate action in response. We collected all the *Outlook* issues we could find and placed them in a hastily constructed wooden coffin. We then tied a black band on our left arms, put a *tarboush* on the coffin, and walked in a mock funeral procession from the Engineering building to the Jafith Library. After we had gathered in front of the library, three of our students delivered obituary speeches criticising *Outlook* and the School of Arts and Sciences. Our 'funeral' demonstration drew a great deal of attention on campus, which more than made up for the joke that had been played on the Engineering School. To this day, engineering students at AUB hold an annual 'Tarboush Day' celebration in honour of our counter-prank.

As the academic year came to an end, the Dean of Engineering invited all the engineering students who were graduating in June 1957 to a special party at his residence. In addition, the President of the AUB Alumni Association, Emile Bustani, invited all graduating students to a special dinner held at the AUB Alumni Club. Acting President Dr Constantine Zureik and senior members of the university faculty also attended this dinner.

Mr Bustani and his wife, Laura, welcomed us at the door and shook hands with all the invitees. For me this was a great event because it was the first time I had met such important personalities. Meeting Emile Bustani was a special thrill for me because he was a well-known member of the Lebanese Parliament and also Chairman of the CAT Company. CAT had directly aided my own education by assisting me with their Loan-in-Aid fund during the last two years of my studies. Shortly after meeting Mr Bustani, I went to work for CAT.

Graduation was a great occasion for my parents and brought me a tremendous sense of satisfaction and feelings of joy. My brother Antoine graduated the same day with a degree as Doctor of Medicine. For my parents, graduation was a double celebration. Our relatives and the people of our village shared my family's joy. In fact, I was the first engineer and my brother was the first doctor to come from Deddeh. Later that year when my brother, Abdallah, received his Baccalaureate degree from the French section of AUB, people from our village said to him: 'When are you going to become an engineer or a doctor like your brothers?'

On Commencement Day two bus loads of people from our village travelled to Beirut to attend our graduation ceremony. My greatest satisfaction was to see my parents and my grandfather among the crowd. After the ceremony, we all went to Deddeh, where the next day we began a full week of celebrations. Many were those visitors who came to our home to congratulate my parents and wish us well. All that has happened – the euphoria of my parents as a result of their children's success; the graduation ceremonies which seemed for the people of my village at least a national event; and finally, the realisation on my part of the possibilities open to me – made me aware that I had reached a milestone in my journey through life.

CHAPTER 4

The Start of My Working Life in Pakistan

In July 1957, I reported to the head office of the Contracting and Trading Company (CAT) in Saifi, Beirut, to begin my career as a professional engineer. There I met with Chief Engineer Nicola Halaby. A Palestinian by birth, Nicola Halaby was a graduate of Loughborough University, UK. On account of his much gained experience working for British firms in Palestine, he was selected by CAT to be the company's Chief Engineer with full jurisdiction over all its working sites. Nicola Halaby was around fifty years old, spoke English with an Oxford accent, and loved to smoke his pipe.

As I sat across from his desk, Nicola Halaby puffed on his pipe, looked me straight in the eye, and asked, 'In which country would you prefer to work?'

I replied, 'Iraq is my choice.'

'There is no vacancy in any of our projects in Iraq at present but how about Kuwait?' he replied.

I said 'No,' without hesitation and I added, 'Nor to any other Arab country like the Trucial States (Bahrain, Qatar, or the UAE).'

'Would you go to Pakistan?' he asked.

Without a second thought I answered, 'Certainly.'

He then specified the terms of my employment: I would be paid L.L.550 per month and would receive a 50 per cent expatriation allowance plus free accommodation and travel. The duration of the contract, renewable by mutual agreement, was for one year with fifteen days holiday.

Having agreed to the terms suggested, the employment department was instructed to prepare my contract and process my travel arrangements. A couple of days before leaving for Pakistan, I went to see Nicola Halaby so that he could brief me on my duties and responsibilities. He told me that he expected to receive favourable reports about my performance from the Project Manager in Pakistan. If my performance reports were positive, I might be granted a bonus at the end of my contract. The report would also have a significant bearing on my future promotion within the company and on subsequent salary increases.

As I left Mr Halaby's office thinking about my new assignment, I remembered Nacerine Jean, a Pakistani student I had met at AUB. She was an Arts and Sciences major on a one-year scholarship sponsored by the Pakistani government. She returned to Karachi at the end of the academic year in June 1957. Before leaving Beirut, she gave me her address and telephone number so that I might contact her if I ever visited her country.

In July 1957, I went to Karachi with a colleague, Zaki Shammas, who graduated from AUB with a degree in Civil Engineering. We flew via British Overseas Airway Corporation (BOAC), now better known as British Airways (BA), on a non-stop, eight-hour flight in a Lockheed Super Constellation. It was an exciting flight: departure from Beirut in the evening and arrival in Karachi at dawn the next day. We were met at the airport by one of the company's employees who drove us to a hotel in town.

At midday, the same driver returned to take us to the main office to meet Mr Roy Beaven, our company's Area Manager, who briefed us on our job assignments. We were to work on a project building a large cantonment for the Pakistani army in the district of Gujrat. We were to travel to the work area at Kahrian near Jhelam by train, a long journey that normally took twenty-eight hours.

When I returned to the hotel I telephoned Nacerine Jean, who was very pleased to hear that I was in town. She came to the hotel with her brother and took us on a brief tour of the city. Dinner that night at a local restaurant was my first introduction to hot and spicy food.

Karachi was a crowded city, highly polluted, and very dirty. Most of the public and private transportation was run by diesel engines and, to my surprise, a large number of motorcycles and bicycles were used as taxis, referred to as *tonga*.

Pakistan emerged as an independent country in 1947, when the Indian subcontinent as a whole gained independence from Britain. The Muslims of the subcontinent were united under the leadership of Mohammed Ali Jinneh, and they sought a separate, independent Muslim state. The British acceded to Muslim demands, and Pakistan was created, against the will of Mahatma Gandhi, to include Bengal

(East Pakistan) and Sind and Punjab (West Pakistan), a united state geographically separated into two halves by newly independent India. In 1971, East Pakistan seceded from Pakistan to form its own independent state, known thereafter as Bangladesh.

As scheduled, I left Karachi by train with my friend Zaki. The trip through the well-known city of Lahore took us to Lalamusa, the nearest train station to our project site at Kahrian. Due to heavy monsoon rains, the trip took longer than usual. For our thirty-two-hour trip, we sat in a very crowded train on wooden seats in second class, sweltering from the heat and humidity. We declined to eat the food that was offered to us, preferring to have tea and biscuits. This trip was a fascinating experience because I was able to see the countryside with its many villages and small hamlets.

We arrived at Lalamusa station totally exhausted and disoriented. On the platform, a man held a large notice with our names written on it. We went to him and introduced ourselves. He immediately asked a porter to take our luggage to the company car, which was waiting nearby. We followed our guide and he drove us in a Land Rover to the company's campsite. Upon arrival, we were each assigned a bedroom in a barracks consisting of brick walls, wooden roof, hardboard false ceilings, and a concrete floor. From the centre of the ceiling of the room hung down a fan which provided scant relief from the extreme heat and humidity.

Toilets and showers were located in the middle room of this twenty-bedroom barracks. We slept that evening after having dinner in the mess hall with some fifteen Lebanese expatriates who were already working on the project. I woke up in the morning to find that the floor of my room was covered by an inch of water from a heavy rainstorm. This flooding revealed the deficiencies of the barracks building we occupied.

Zaki and I finally reached the project office at 8:00 in the morning where we met the company's agent, Fuad Hajj. Fuad, a graduate engineer from a British university, had worked with CAT for some seven years on projects in Aden and Kuwait before taking his current post. He briefed us on the project and explained our company's obligations to our client, the Oman Farnsworth Wright (OFW) joint venture.

Our project, as I mentioned, was to construct an army cantonment to accommodate a full brigade of approximately 30,000 officers and enlisted men. The project was funded by the US Department of Defense and was under the overall supervision of the US Army Corps of Engineers. The main contractor, which by US law had to be American, was a joint venture by Oman of Tennessee and Farnsworth & Wright of California. The consulting engineering company was also American, Dumont Greer of Washington, DC.

Because Pakistan had recently achieved independence from Britain, OFW decided to employ British sub-contractors. Gammon Engineers was selected for the construction of buildings, CAT for the mechanical and external utilities, GEC (General Electric Company) for internal electrical utilities, and Henley Cables for the high- and low-tension electrical distribution system. OFW itself constructed roads, parking lots, and an airstrip.

The cantonment spread over an area of eight square kilometres and was located at Kahrian, in the district of Gujrat, around 145 kilometres north of Lahore on the road to Rawalpindi. Each company built a temporary camp and compound near the cantonment to accommodate its expatriate staff. It was expected that the project would be completed in three years. The American compound was the largest and best organised. It had both family and bachelor quarters. The other two compounds, those of Gammon and CAT, were smaller and built to a lower standard. Adjacent to the boundary line of the American compound was a club that catered to all expatriates working on the project. It was called the 'Carry-On Club' and had an English pub, an American cocktail lounge, a spacious reception hall, and a gaming room for cards, pool, and ping-pong. The club also featured an outdoor swimming pool, two tennis courts, and an open air cinema. Later, tracks for go-carts and horse racing were added.

Expatriates who wished to join the 'Carry-On Club' paid a small monthly membership fee. A board of governors was elected to manage the club's affairs. No less than seventeen different nationalities worked on the project, namely Americans, Canadians, British, Irish, Germans, French, Danes, Italians, Portuguese, Spanish, Lebanese, Palestinians, Jordanians, Syrians, Australians, Japanese, and Filipinos. Over 200 expatriate engineers and technicians lived and worked in this small multi national community, and about a quarter of them had families with them. Each nationality kept its own traditions: the Americans, for example, celebrated Thanksgiving and Halloween;

the Irish, St Patrick's Day; and the French, Bastille Day. Each group prepared its own national foods and drank its traditional drinks. I was proud that at the 'Carry-On Club', Lebanese dishes were most popular and in great demand.

For me, at the age of twenty-two, it was quite an experience to come from Lebanon and begin working on a project with such a strong and varied international team. I had a lot to learn in a very short time. Fuad Hajj appointed me as Site Engineer for plumbing. In addition, I was given responsibility for refrigeration and kitchen equipment in the mess halls of the enlisted men and junior officers. To facilitate my work, I was assigned a Jeep and driver to take me around the scattered locations for which I was responsible. One expatriate foreman and three artisan plumbers assisted me in my work. In addition, a design engineer and two draftsmen helped by preparing all of our working drawings. Local Pakistani labourers were recruited, but they required training before they could start working. Plumbing is the most difficult trade in the building industry, and we faced a challenge because skilled plumbers simply were not available in Pakistan at that time. We could easily find a mason or a carpenter, but not a plumber. Fortunately, the training of competent plumbers proved to be relatively easy because our Pakistani labourers were hard-working and eager to learn.

Training was not our only challenge. Detailed drawings had to be prepared and approved by the Corps of Engineers and material orders had to be placed. We tried to time deliveries to coincide with the partial completion of buildings so that our plumbers could install pipes and fittings. Co-ordination between the building sub-contractor, Gammon, and the plumbing crew was essential. Our client required a great deal of preparatory input at the beginning of the project – work for which the contractor received no compensation because payment was based on the completion of each section of the project. This was a somewhat unfair arrangement.

Inspection of our work, both in the office and on-site, was strict and uncompromising. At the time, the project as a whole was under the control of the Area Engineer of the US Corps of Engineers, Colonel Sneitzer. A Security and Safety Officer from the US Army, an Area Construction Superintendent from OFW, the Contractor, and a Resident Engineer from Dumont Greer consultants, assisted the Colonel. A Mechanical Superintendent, Simon Delatte, assisted

The Start of My Working Life in Pakistan

the Area Superintendent, Sam Bradley, who was responsible for all the work done by our company, CAT. Greer and the consultants were represented by their Resident Engineer, William Boutwell, who was in charge of field inspection.

Regular monthly meetings were held, presided over by the Area Engineer and attended by the Resident Engineer, the Security Officer, the Area Superintendent, and the senior representatives of the four sub-contractors (Gammon, CAT, GEC, and Henley Cables). Weekly meetings were also held between the OFW Area Superintendent and representatives of the sub-contractors to review progress, co-ordinate work, and solve problems.

When I started working on the project I had to familiarise myself with the scope of my responsibilities. To do this, I read the project's specification book and reviewed all the relevant contract drawings. I followed this research by reviewing field drawings and material take-off in the engineering office. I also surveyed material procurement orders with the Chief Storekeeper, Wadie Ghabriel. At the same time, I was introduced to Simon Delatte of OFW and Richard Sterling of the Corps of Engineers along with their supervisors and inspectors. These gentlemen regularly came to our office to discuss issues with Fuad Hajj.

Complaints about lack of supervisory staff and shortage of materials were lodged, and Fuad defended our company by sharing his perspective on the progress of our work. With many problems to solve, I started visiting the site on a daily basis. In this way, I gained insight into the real cause of our problems. Shortage of materials was as detrimental to our progress as was lack of proper drawings and trained plumbers and fitters. In addition, delays by the plumbing crew directly affected progress by the building sub-contractor, Gammon, who in turn reported us to the main contractor. Many exchanges took place between my plumbing unit and the electrical sub-contractors. For example, no concrete slab could be poured before the three sub-contractors, the main contractor, and the Corps of Engineers inspector had each signed a permission slip. Such a system had never been used before by any of the contractors and was deemed to be strict, demanding, and time consuming.

My company experienced many problems on this project, but in fairness it should be noted that Pakistan was a new environment for us; the other contractors, in contrast, had been established on the subcontinent for many years before us.

CAT was under constant pressure from the main contractor, OFW, to get organised and meet all project requirements. As the Site Engineer, I was first in line to face such pressures. I faced an uphill struggle because I was not able to get my management to provide the required materials and trained plumbers on time. Challenges occurred because most materials had to be imported from the United States, and final orders could not be placed until working drawings were prepared and approved by the Corps of Engineers. This was a time consuming process that could take weeks or even months.

My friend Zaki Shammas was experiencing the same sort of problems with his job of laying water lines and sewers. We often exchanged ideas and opinions about our difficulties, both during and after working hours. To complicate matters further, the standard of living that CAT employees experienced in the camp was poor, much lower than that enjoyed by the staff of OFW and Gammon. We had no air-conditioning in our dormitories, just ceiling fans that did nothing to cool the air or control the humidity. There was no leisure centre, no lounge with reading material, no music system. We raised these problems, both verbally and in writing, on many occasions with Fuad Hajj, but nothing happened.

Faced with an unbearable situation, Zaki and I submitted our resignations in early November 1957 and requested immediate repatriation to Beirut. Fuad Hajj tried to persuade us to stay, but without success. With no other choice, he gave each of us 200 rupees to cover the cost of a train fare to Karachi. Furthermore, he said that Roy Beaven, the Project Manager in Karachi, would make arrangements for our trip to Beirut. A third person, George Haddad, a Technical Assistant, joined us and we left for Karachi in mid-November.

Upon our arrival in Karachi the next day, I telephoned Mr Beaven to inform him that we were staying at the Central Hotel. I asked him if he would be kind enough to arrange our travel to Beirut. He asked us to stay in the hotel until he contacted us again. Two days later, he telephoned to say that he had news from Beirut for Zaki and me. He asked us to come to his office for a meeting.

When we arrived at Roy Beaven's office, he began the conversation by saying that he had received definite instructions from

The Start of My Working Life in Pakistan

the Chairman of our company, Emile Bustani, that we should return to the job site. Furthermore, Emile Bustani assured us that he would personally ensure that our demands were met. Roy Beaven reported that Emile Bustani was scheduled to visit Pakistan in person in December and planned to meet with us to discuss our concerns. He went on to say that he had started taking action to improve conditions. He said that Fuad Hajj would be transferred to Karachi and would be replaced by Edward Roberts. Roy Beaven also assured us, saying, 'On your return to the site you'll implement a two-fold plan: first, to improve the accommodation for our expatriates; and second, to prepare a new organisation and progress chart for the project that will be satisfactory to our client. We'll support you from here to achieve this plan and I'm appointing Mr Hajj solely to expedite procurement of material and recruitment of staff.'

Faced with prospects of improvement, we agreed to go back to the job site. I remember the day of our return vividly because it was my introduction to the American holiday of Thanksgiving, which was celebrated with a dinner held in the 'Carry-On Club'. On arrival at the club, there were cries and shouts from several people saying, 'Welcome back boys! We're very happy you're back!' I felt wonderful and was happy that we took the right decisions, both in leaving and in returning.

The next day we reported to the project's main office and resumed our work, this time according to the plan we had worked out with Roy Beaven in Karachi. We began by starting construction of a new compound to provide better accommodation for our staff. I took responsibility for internal utilities and procurement and Zaki took responsibility for external utilities. More support for our efforts was forthcoming, both from Beirut and Karachi, and in two months I was able to assert my authority. As a result of these changes, we achieved much better progress. The client, OFW, and the Corps of Engineers were impressed and also extended their full support.

Towards the end of 1957, Emile Bustani, the Chairman of our company, fulfilled his promise and visited our work site with the OFW Project Manager, Rodney Mims, who had come all the way from New York. During a special meeting late in the evening with Zaki and myself, Emile Bustani expressed his gratitude for our willingness to continue working on the project. 'Look,' he said, 'you are still young and there's much for you to learn. It's now the time to do so and look forward to the future. With engineers like you in the company there will be a bright future for all. I'll be gone but the company will be there for you and generations to follow. So persevere, keep up the good work, and please write to me directly in case you have any problems.' The next day he began his trip back to Beirut by way of Karachi.

From that day forward, I carried out my work with full confidence in myself. All concerned parties appreciated my performance. The Corps of Engineers inspectors and OFW supervisors commended me for the progress achieved and expressed their opinion to my agent, Edward Roberts. I maintained a good working relationship with both my expatriate staff and our local Pakistani labourers. Outside working hours, I managed to associate with members of the construction community despite the many nationalities that were represented. I saw to it that we, as Lebanese, learned from the Americans and Europeans. At the same time, we Lebanese enjoyed a great opportunity to introduce our way of life to our European and American counterparts. A new atmosphere of co-operation prevailed throughout the project, extending even to the families on site.

Colonel Sneitzer of the Corps of Engineers monitored overall progress through an Executive Committee composed of the top people working on the project. For social and civic functions, he relied on a respected person drawn from each of the various expatriate communities. These arrangements fostered an environment of contentment.

By January 1958, the re-organisation of the project was completed. Senior personnel included Edward Roberts, Farid Khoursheed, Eric Devereux, myself, and my friend Zaki Shammas. Our labour force totalled around 600, with approximately 50 expatriates of Lebanese, Jordanian, Palestinian, and British nationality.

Typically, my workday began at 6:00 a.m. when I woke up. By 7:00 a.m., I was touring the site to check on progress and to identify problems. I returned to my office at around 10:00 a.m. to review technical drawings and to place orders for needed materials. The same cycle was repeated after lunch. I returned to camp around 7:00 p.m. We worked six days a week, but in some cases we also worked a seventh day (on Sundays). After three months of intensive efforts, my wishes were fulfilled: the project was progressing according to plan, materials were arriving on site on schedule, and the number of expatriates had been increased. The Corps of Engineers and OFW expressed their satisfaction and commended my company on the improvements that had been made.

In October 1957 my family moved to Beirut, where they occupied a rented flat on Hamra Street. My eldest brother, Antoine, had left to work in New York, where he had obtained an internship in abdominal and vascular surgery at Upstate Medical Center in the city of Syracuse. At this time, my brother Abdallah was attending AUB, and all of my five other brothers and sisters were enrolled in various schools in Beirut. Besides my father, I was the only breadwinner in the family. My father visited Beirut on the weekends but spent weekdays in Deddeh attending to his business. His income was much lower than the family's living and educational expenses. He sold properties and borrowed against others in an attempt to make ends meet. In short, my father relied heavily on my income to solve our family's financial situation. At the end of each month, I transferred my entire salary to my brother Abdallah. He, in turn, sent me letters detailing how the money was spent on items like tuition, rent, and other expenses.

In July 1958, I visited Beirut during my fifteen-days' yearly leave. Upon arriving, I found that Lebanon was wracked by political upheaval. This coincided with the Iraqi revolution that toppled King Faisal and his Prime Minister, Nouri Al-Assaed. In the midst of this regional disruption, the United States decided to send a force of Marines into Beirut. Under these circumstances, I decided to cut my holiday short and return to Pakistan.

In September of the same year, my friend and colleague Zaki developed a serious illness, and our company decided to send him to Beirut for urgent treatment. As a result, I was asked to take over his job in addition to my own. I now became Site Engineer for both internal and external utilities. Later, the Beirut office sent two engineers to assist me, Marwan Khartabil and Basim Azzam. I immediately put Marwan in charge of external utilities and gave Basim responsibility for internal utilities. Marwan was a recent graduate of Loughborough University in Britain and Basim had just finished his studies at Roberts College in Istanbul.

Marwan was keen to learn about construction and devoted extra efforts to this end. Basim, in contrast, wanted to learn but was not prepared to do extra duty. Obviously, I was happy with Marwan's performance but dissatisfied with that of Basim. Marwan, who became a very good friend of mine, left after a year to take a Master's degree in Civil Engineering at Cornell University in the United States. Basim continued to work at CAT until the 1960s, when he started his own business in Abu Dhabi. Marwan's intention was to take his Master's degree and return to CAT to work on projects under my direct supervision.

Thereafter, he expressed his intention to Emile Bustani on several occasions. Marwan corresponded with me throughout the following two years until we met again in Beirut in December 1962 after his graduation from Cornell. Meanwhile, in December 1959 Edward Roberts resigned his post as agent and returned to London; Eric Devereux took over his job. By this time the project was approximately 60 per cent complete, and our company was contemplating bidding on another contract to build another army cantonment in Multan, a major city in West Pakistan. The award came through in mid-1959, and the company decided to transfer Eric Devereux to act as agent there. While the company searched for a British national to replace Eric Devereux, they asked me to serve as engineer-in-charge until the arrival of a new agent. The search for a new agent presented difficulties, and for a four-month period I performed the job to the satisfaction of OFW and the Corps of Engineers. When the new appointee finally arrived in Karachi, he was soon asked to return to Beirut and the Project Manager in Karachi, Fuad Hajj, then appointed me as agent. Shortly thereafter, I received a letter from Emile Bustani in which he complimented me on my work and congratulated me on my promotion.

Apparently, Rodney Mims, the Project Manager for OFW, had written a letter to Emile Bustani commending my work as engineer-in-charge and requesting him not to rock the boat and appoint me as agent. Emile Bustani was delighted because this turn of events strengthened his hand as he sought to convince the Chairman of the Motherwell Bridge and Engineering Company that Arab engineers could, in time, replace British personnel, and at a much lower cost. The cost savings would give their partnership, called Mothercat, better profit margins and make them more competitive when bidding on projects.

The Start of My Working Life in Pakistan

I managed the project for about six months, until it was approximately 90 per cent complete. In May 1960, I moved to Multan to take over as agent from Eric Devereux, who was transferred to London. During the last few months of my stay in Kahrian, I began my first work in pipeline construction. My company was contracted by Attock Oil Company to construct 115 kilometres of a crude oil pipeline running from the Dulian fields to the refinery in Rawalpindi. Faiz Boustany, General Manager of the pipeline construction division in Beirut asked me to take charge of this project because of its proximity (about 150 kilometres) to Kahrian. This arrangement suited me because it was a new challenge.

To supervise the pipeline construction project, I visited the project's base camp three times a week to meet with the superintendent, foremen, and welders – all of whom were Lebanese or Arabs from other countries. I reported problems and progress to Beirut on a weekly and monthly basis. The job, including testing and commissioning, was completed in six months. Our client was very satisfied and expressed this sentiment in the certificate of completion. I had built good working relations with the pipeline team of foremen, welders, and other artisans. My performance on this job prompted Faiz Boustany in Beirut to request my transfer to the pipeline division of our company. Also, I was to be appointed manager of pipeline projects in the Gulf States. However, the management refused Faiz Boustany's request because I was already slated to take over as agent for Multan. I must admit that, although I took a liking to pipeline construction, I preferred to continue working on the military projects.

I moved to Multan with Marwan Khartabil (Site Engineer), and Wadie Ghabriel (Administrator). Friends from the Corps of Engineers, OFW, Gammon, and others gave several farewell dinner parties at the 'Carry-On Club' or at their homes. Lebanese and Pakistani staff of CAT threw a party in a large tent erected specially for the occasion. Invited guests included senior Pakistani officers from the Gujrat district in addition to expatriates and senior Pakistani staff involved in the project.

*   *   *

Multan is a major city located in the mid-western region of what was then West Pakistan. Mango and citrus farms surround the city, which is the hottest location in the country with temperatures varying between 15°C and 43°C.

The cantonment we were contracted to build was located on the western edge of the city. At the same time, Mothercat was constructing a new power station on the eastern side of Multan. Also, a consortium of French companies was building a fertiliser plant in the vicinity. Most of the staff working on the cantonment were transferred from our project at Kahrian. The Corps of Engineers and OFW staffs were accommodated in their own compound specially built for the project, as were the Gammon and GEC staffs. We, however, were accommodated in private, rented houses in the city.

Work at Multan was easier to cope with because it was essentially an extension of what we had done at Kahrian. Therefore, no major problems were encountered. The same procedures and systems were applied and the staff was well trained to execute them. Procurement of materials from abroad was also made easier by the mere fact that we utilised the same suppliers. Wadie Ghabriel, Marwan Khartabil, and Alexi Majdalani constituted the core of my expatriate staff. Their dedication to my system of work made it possible to achieve a high rate of progress. The site was impressive because this cantonment was an extension to an existing one built during the time of British rule. The site contained high trees, flower plantations, and thick vegetation.

Social life in Multan was more pleasant than it had been in Kahrian. We were able to build relationships with expatriates working on other projects and also with prominent local Pakistanis. I had the opportunity to form a friendship with George T. Talia, an Iraqi national who had lived most of his life in India before the partition. George was well known to Emile Bustani because they had studied together at AUB in the 1930s. Emile Bustani was the Chairman of CAT and Deputy Chairman of Mothercat. CAT was considered a British company due to its partnership with Motherwell Engineering of Scotland in a company called Mothercat. Since Mothercat was classified as a British company, the chairmanship was held by Motherwell Bridge. But since their work was mainly in the Middle East, the Deputy Chairman had the effective ability to run the company from his offices in Beirut. In 1955 George Talia was employed as an administrator in Karachi when Mothercat began

The Start of My Working Life in Pakistan

constructing the SuiGas pipeline. He left this job in 1957 after a disagreement with management, but maintained good relations with Mothercat's Deputy Chairman.

To make use of George Talia's knowledge of, and experience in, Pakistan, Emile Bustani agreed to form a company with him for the sole purpose of providing aggregate and sand to contractors. Their first contract was with Mothercat for the power station project at Multan. Aggregate and sand were moved several hundred kilometres from their source to the work site via rail wagons. It was essential to obtain the required wagons from the railway. George Talia maintained excellent relations with the railway, so he was able to execute orders and make deliveries on time. He secured two additional contracts for Gammon, the defence project I was working on, and the nearby fertiliser plant (being built by French contractors).

Towards the beginning of 1961 the work on the cantonment was virtually complete, and I was transferred to Karachi to take over as Project Manager of the civil works of Pakistan Refinery Ltd (PRL) at Korangi. PRL was a partnership between the government of Pakistan and a group of foreign oil companies (led by Shell of The Hague) to build a refinery. Shell was the engineer and Kellogg International was the main contractor to PRL. Mothercat was the sub-contractor for the civil works, a responsibility that entailed moving a considerable quantity of earth to raise the refinery site by an average of two metres above ground level. Fill material was transported from a borrow pit five kilometres away which was connected by a metalled road that ran from Karachi to a Pakistani Air Force base at Korangi.

Our heavy earth moving equipment used for transporting fill material was restricted to a private road alongside the main road. This arrangement was designed to protect the metalled road from damage, but because we were working three shifts a day, the night operators used the metalled road and did in fact damage its surface. As a result, the Commander of the air base sent a strongly worded letter of complaint to PRL and the Pakistani Highways and Roads Department. The Resident Engineer, Mr Goodsy (a Shell appointee from The Hague), called the Project Manager of Kellogg and myself to an urgent meeting in his office to discuss the situation. As a result of that meeting, we were instructed to cease our earth moving operation until I met with the Air Force Commander to agree on a plan for repairing the road. This plan was to be communicated in writing to PRL before Goodsy would allow us to resume work.

As agreed, I met with the Commander and pledged that we would repair the road at our expense upon completion of our work one month later; alternatively, we would pay the Pakistani government in cash to cover the cost of repairs. I presented this agreement to Goodsy, who allowed us to resume work on the condition that none of our equipment used the metalled road. I agreed to this condition, saying that I would instruct the operators not to use the metalled road under threat of a heavy penalty. A few days later, Goodsy visited the site at 3:00 a.m. and discovered one of our tournapouls (a piece of heavy equipment, also called a 'scraper') running on the metalled road. In response, he issued an order at 8:00 a.m. to Kellogg to cease all work; he also wanted an emergency meeting at his office.

The Project Manager of Kellogg, who was seriously concerned about this matter, conveyed the news to me and requested my presence at the meeting. We went together to PRL and met with Goodsy and his Chief Engineer. I was totally ignored during the meeting by Goodsy, who addressed his words to the other gentlemen without even looking at me. In fact, I tried to intercede in the discussion to offer my opinion, but was not given a chance. I felt very insulted and lost my patience.

I stood up, looked Goodsy straight in the eye, and said, 'A few days ago I obtained for you an agreement with the Commander of the base on the use of the road and said we would provide compensation for any damage.'

Goodsy interrupted me, and in great anger stated, 'I don't care what you agreed with the Commander. I ordered you not to use the road and you did not obey my orders.'

Then as I walked towards the door I replied, 'If that's the case, get ready to pay for our idle equipment and idle time. Our invoices will be at your desk every morning. I'll leave you now, gentlemen, because you'll not listen to anything I say.'

I left, and two hours later the Chief Engineer of Kellogg, Robert Struthers, called me on the telephone to say that we should meet to arrange a plan for resuming work. We did so, and the job was completed in May 1961.

In July of that same year, I took a holiday after three years of continuous work. I went on a European tour with my friend Wadie

The Start of My Working Life in Pakistan

Ghabriel during which we visited four capital cities: London, Amsterdam, Copenhagen, and Vienna. We spent five days in each city and we made the best of our short visits. In London, we saw some friends we had met in Pakistan. They showed us around the high spots in the city like the museums, the Changing of the Guard at Buckingham Palace, Petticoat Lane, and other interesting sites. In the evenings we visited places like Lyceum Hall and saw shows such as 'My Fair Lady' and 'The Music Man'.

In Amsterdam we visited the Red Light District and the Rembrandt Museum. In Copenhagen, we spent evenings at the Tivoli Gardens, where we met and danced with girls of different nationalities. We took the famous Danube river-boat tour at night in Vienna, and we visited the Central City Park where Johann Strauss' music was played live throughout the day. All in all, it was an enjoyable holiday full of excitement and surprises that I can still recall to this day.

Upon my return to Beirut, I found two telegrams from Faiz Boustany requesting my immediate attendance at the company's head office to arrange for my travel to Karachi. When we met at the office, Faiz said to me, 'We've been asked by Kellogg to give them a price for constructing three pipelines to be laid in one trench extending from the port at Kimari to the PRL refinery at Korangi. The lines will each be six, nine, and twelve inches in diameter and 27 kilometres in length.' Faiz went on to say, 'I'm sending our Chief Estimator, Jack Verhak, from Beirut to visit the site, inspect the right of way, and estimate the cost of the project. As you're going to be the Project Manager, I want you to be with Jack from the start to prepare the right price for this job. As time is short, I'll follow you in ten days to submit the final estimates to Kellogg and hopefully negotiate and sign a contract.'

The route of the pipeline extended along the seashore over very unusual terrain. It crossed a wet section around six kilometres from the boundary wall of the refinery with two sea water creeks, 200 and 450 metres wide respectively. Somewhere in the middle of the pipeline, at a place called Clifton Bay, there was a two kilometre section of sand dunes. As we approached the port of Kimari, the area became more industrial, with many utility crossings and buildings.

Having surveyed the proposed route of the pipeline, my colleague Jack Verhak decided that our company should not take this job, and so he informed Faiz Boustany who was still in Beirut. Contrary to what Jack Verhak believed, I thought that the job could be done and I expressed this opinion to our superiors. When he heard my report, Faiz Boustany looked at me and said, 'I know you can do it but I'm scared.' I replied without hesitation, 'Please take the job and don't worry.' We agreed on what the estimated cost of the project should be, and two weeks later a contract was signed. I was appointed Project Manager. Kellogg did not object to my appointment, but PRL in the name of Goodsy did.

Undeterred by Goodsy's objection, I immediately mobilised a crew and began working on the project. Within a month, we were moving pipes from a supply yard and stringing them along the route of the pipeline. Welders and equipment arrived from Beirut and Kuwait by the middle of November. Amidst all this, the Chief Engineer of Kellogg told me, 'We have to resolve the problem of your appointment with Goodsy. He is totally against your involvement.' He went on to say, 'I'm writing to your management in Beirut to arrange for a replacement.'

'Please go ahead,' I replied, 'and undoubtedly I will be in touch with Beirut regarding this matter as well.' A few days later, I received a telegram from Beirut advising me that Faiz Boustany would arrive in Karachi the next day. I met him at the airport at 4:00 a.m. and took him to his hotel. We did not speak very much because when I saw him I detected signs of rage on his face. All he asked me was, 'What time is my meeting with Kellogg and PRL?' I told him 11:00 a.m. I was with John McMillan, our Area Manager, when Faiz returned from that meeting. He looked at me and said, 'What have you done that has angered Goodsy so much?'

I replied, 'All I said and did was in the interest of the job and my company.'

Faiz continued: 'Yes, but you could've behaved better than addressing him while walking out and saying, "Be ready to pay for the idle time of our equipment and labour!" and then slamming the door behind you.'

John McMillan was quick to add a comment of his own: 'Goodsy is a retired Air Force Commander and he personifies the true character of a Dutch officer.'

'Never mind that,' Faiz said, 'I've apologised on behalf of the company, and I've stressed that George is the best man for the job.

We agreed to turn over a new leaf in our dealings with Goodsy, so please, George, be very tactful.'

I replied, 'Faiz, you had better find a replacement because I cannot continue to work under such pressure.'

His reply was swift and to the point, 'George, please do not start this again. Remember your commitment to me when we negotiated the contract. It's your job and you have to do it.'

For yet another time in my working life, I felt I was under intense pressure. I was in a hole that I had dug for myself by behaving the way I did with Goodsy, and now I had to get myself out of it. No one could help me with this task. I faced a great challenge, and I set myself on the road to deal with the difficult situation. I took a flat in a building at Clifton Hill, almost halfway between Kimari and Korangi. This served as both my accommodation and my project office. For a period of five months, between November 1961 and March 1962, I worked continuously, except for those hours I was in bed sleeping. After daylight working hours ended, I joined the foremen, welders, and fitters on site to resolve problems and to plan the following day's work. My relationship with the inspectors of Kellogg and PRL was of great importance to me.

The PRL inspector was brought into the project from retirement. He had a great deal of experience working in the American state of Louisiana, and so was an expert in laying pipelines in swampy terrain. The same applied to the Kellogg inspector, who was from the city of Nashville in the American state of Tennessee. In general, these two inspectors praised our performance and progress. However, we strongly differed on the method of laying the lines across two creeks. After much discussion, we solved the problem of the 200-metre long crossing across the first creek by laying the lines over a bridge specially constructed from concrete piles and steel cross beams. But it was not possible to apply the same method to cross the second creek because we could not position either heavy or light equipment closer than 300 metres from each bank. I came to the conclusion that, under the circumstances, there was only one solution: we had to create an earth fill dam across the creek and extend it on both sides to make a right-of-way accessible to our pipe laying equipment.

To implement my plan, we had to move around 100,000 cubic metres of earth without using any mechanical equipment or dump trucks. Therefore, we had to resort to a primitive method: donkeys. Following an enquiry by my local staff, I made contact with four donkey contractors who were able to supply us with 2,000 of these beasts. Naturally the use of donkeys invited a great deal of mockery and criticism from both Shell's and Kellogg's inspectors. Despite the derision, after two months of continuous work we completed the job of crossing the second creek and moved on with the project. We finished all work by the end of March.

One day while I was with the Shell inspector supervising the last tie-in with the refinery pipe intake, Goodsy made a surprise visit. He stopped his car, came straight up to me, and said, 'Mr Zakhem, my congratulations. I want to thank you for a job very well done.' I received his compliment with great satisfaction and saw it as a reward for my relentless efforts. To his credit, I came to understand later that he wrote to our management in Beirut in the same vein. In addition, he went on record with Shell in The Hague stating that I was a highly qualified engineer in pipeline construction and recommended me for future Shell projects. In fact, ten years later (in 1972) my company, Zakhem International Construction, tendered for a job with Qatar Petroleum Co. (QPC) to lay a 130-kilometre gas pipeline. We were the lowest bidders, coming in at 15 per cent below the second-lowest contractor, CAT. Shell was the engineering firm for QPC, and strongly endorsed our bid. The job was awarded to us in full confidence that we could perform at the price we had quoted, on the recommendation given by Goodsy to the project team in The Hague.

CHAPTER 5

The Beginnings of an Independent Professional Career in Lebanon

By early April 1962, I concluded that I was not being properly rewarded for my work with CAT, so I tendered my resignation in writing to Faiz Boustany in Beirut, with a copy to Emile Bustani. I gave them three months notice, during which time I carried on my duties as well as the duties of the Area Manager, who had taken an extended holiday. In May, I received a tender for the US Corps of Engineers to perform work at the American Air Force base in Peshawar, work which included constructing an elevated water tank and a sewage treatment plant. In June, I visited Beirut accompanied by George Reed, President of the Mid-East Construction Company (our partners on the job), to finalise the estimated budget for the Peshawar project. While in Beirut, Emile Bustani called me to a special meeting at his office to discuss the business of the company in Pakistan and to ask me why I had resigned. After one hour discussing the present and future business of the company, I was candid with him and said I was not appreciated nor properly compensated by his management team, and that my plan for the future was simply to work on my own. I told Emile that, at the age of twenty-seven, I was still young and could afford to spend five years or so trying to succeed on my own. My brother Abdallah would soon graduate with a degree in Civil Engineering, and he would join me in my future endeavours, whatever they may be.

Emile interrupted me and asked, 'Do you have the money to start your own business? Where will you get it?'

I replied, 'I'll ask my father to sell a piece of land to provide the necessary capital to make a start.'

To my surprise, he responded, 'How about taking me as a "sleeping partner"? I'll provide all the required capital and you'll be the active partner.'

He continued, 'It'll be a partnership between you and me. No one else from CAT will have anything to do with you but me.'

Surprised though I was, I replied, 'It's a great honour to be your partner, Mr Bustani. Yes, I accept.'

Emile Bustani immediately called in his legal advisor and gave him instructions to register a limited liability company with a starting capital of L.L.100,000, equivalent to $35,000. We decided to call the new company HAPICAT (Heating, Air-Conditioning, Piping, Contracting, and Trading). Emile then said, 'Now that we have agreed on things, you should return to Karachi and resume your job as usual for CAT and Mothercat. I'll notify you when the registration of our company is complete.' He added, 'Go immediately now to Duncan Robertson, the General Manager of construction for Mothercat, and inform him that you are going back to Karachi. But remember now which hat to wear when performing your duty.' I mentioned that I would need to take two employees from the CAT staff with me to start up HAPICAT, Wadie Ghabriel and Alexi Majdalani. Emile agreed to this plan.

I walked out from my two-hour meeting with Emile Bustani satisfied with what I had achieved, and proud that I had become his business partner. My partnership with Emile was a major step in the development of my career. A few days later, I left for Karachi and informed all concerned of my new partnership and status. My colleagues were surprised to see me back in Pakistan because I had resigned just two months before. Later I visited Multan to oversee the final phase of construction at the cantonment. As part of demobilisation at that site, I despatched materials and equipment to Peshawar for the new work at the American Air Force base.

We recruited a new expatriate engineer from Beirut, Nadim Majzoub, to take over as Project Engineer at the Peshawar project. I met my colleague George Talia in Multan, and he started telling me about his new venture in the construction industry. In addition to his aggregate and sand supply business, George was negotiating with an Italian-owned contractor – Cogefar Astaldi JV – to build two housing colonies along the Qadrabad-Baluki link canal site. The Water and Power Development Authority (WAPDA), under a special World Bank Aid Program, had just awarded this project to Cogefar Astaldi JV.

The Beginings of an Independent Professional Career in Lebanon

George Talia was at heart an entrepreneur of the highest order. He was an Arab who had lived in Pakistan since the country had achieved independence from Britain. He was well educated and spoke three languages fluently, namely Arabic, English, and Urdu. George was a great expert in public relations, and was well connected with high ranking officials in Pakistan. He entertained his friends in lavish style at his homes at Multan and Rawalpindi. His second wife, Phillis, was an Anglo-Indian who always assisted George in his work. His generosity and hospitality contributed in no small measure to his status. With his background, he succeeded in his first business venture as a supplier of aggregate and sand to contractors. Both materials had to be carried via rail wagons over 645 kilometres from their point of origin to the customers. Obviously, obtaining enough wagons from the North-Western railway was critical to this operation. George Talia's excellent relations with the railway enabled him to obtain the necessary wagons to deliver materials and meet deadlines. CAT and Mothercat were his first customers, followed by other contractors like Gammon Ltd.

While negotiating with Cogefar Astaldi for the supply of aggregate and sand for the Qadrabad-Baluki link canal project, George was told about two housing colonies that were to be built by sub-contractors. He immediately began posing himself as a contractor who could do this work. The Project Manager of Cogefar liked the idea and persuaded his superiors to negotiate with Talia. In the midst of these negotiations, I met Talia in Multan. During our talk, he looked at me in a very unusual manner and said that he had received a letter of complaint from Emile Bustani, blaming him for disrupting relations with CAT and Mothercat and giving preference to Gammon and other contractors. Talia said that Emile Bustani was requesting an explanation. He also said that it was the first time that he (Talia) had received such a letter from Bustani, and that his reply had been harsh.

Talia then pulled out two letters from his pocket – his reply and Bustani's original letter – and showed both letters to me.

He asked, 'Did you tell him anything about me when you were in Beirut?'

I replied, 'Yes. When asked for my opinion about you I said, "Talia works solely for his own interest. If his interest is served better with any of our competitors he will do that without any consideration of our long-term relationship and your personal relationship with him." '

To this, Talia responded, 'Look, George, I'm about to sign a contract with Cogefar to build their housing colonies. I'm going into a joint venture with Gammon and I'll never consider CAT. I don't want anything to do with CAT representatives in this country.'

'How about working with me?' I asked. 'I've just formed a company with Emile called HAPICAT and any agreement would be between you and me.'

Talia thought for a moment and said, 'I accept that proposal, but send a wire to Emile Bustani immediately to get his approval.'

Therefore, I sent the following telegram to Emile in Beirut:

> George Talia embarking on a contract to build two housing colonies for Cogefar Astaldi on Qadrabad-Baluki link canal project stop willing to joint venture with any of your companies excluding CAT and Mothercat stop please cable if you agree to me negotiating on behalf of HAPICAT stop value of contract around two million dollars stop if agreeable depute M. Watkins to come to Karachi to draw up the agreement stop please send your reply to Peshawar stop George Zakhem

After two days I received Emile's reply, which read:

> Agree to your negotiation with Talia stop arranging M. Watkins travel stop please count your fingers after shaking hands with George stop good luck stop Emile Bustani

I immediately called George Talia on the telephone and read the text of the telegram. He replied that he would prove himself to be worthy of Emile's trust.

One week later, I met with Talia and Watkins at the Falettis Hotel in Lahore to finalise our agreement. We decided that the name of the joint venture would be TALIHAP. Fifteen days later, TALIHAP signed a contract with Cogefar Astaldi JV. This event was another milestone in the history of my career.

TALIHAP moved on to the work site of the first colony in August 1962. It was located at Vihari, approximately 130 kilometres to the north-west of Multan. We mobilised material and staff swiftly. I acted as the Project Manager, Wadie Ghabriel as Administrator, and my brother, Abdallah, as Site Engineer. By the end of October

1

2

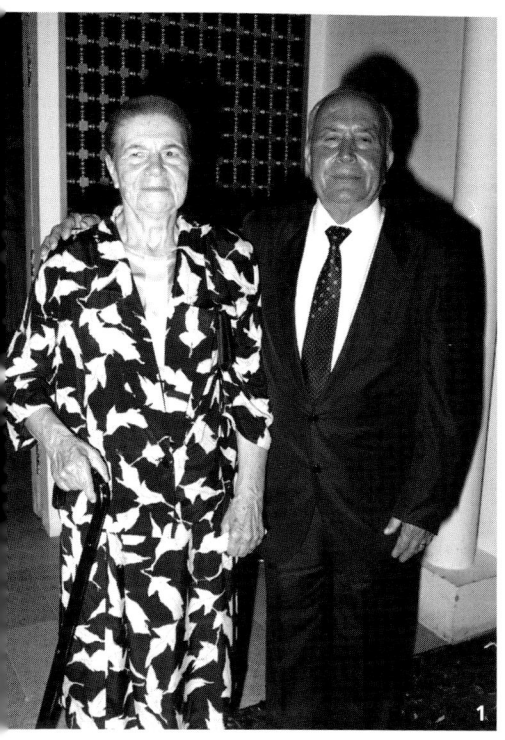

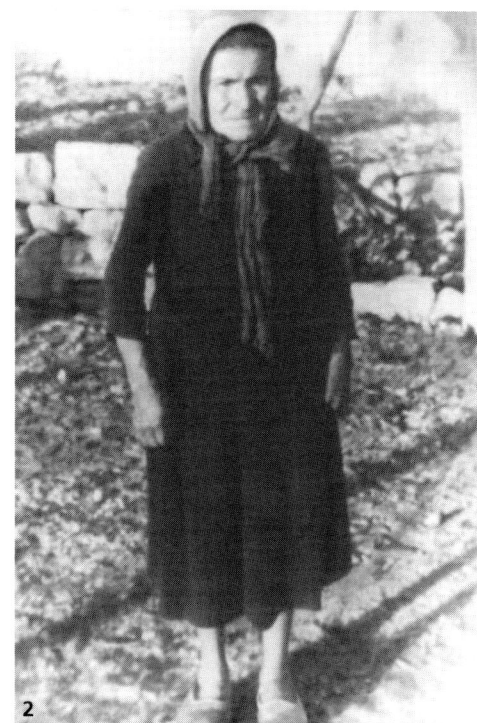

My family

1 My mother and father **2** My grandmother, Tarfa **3** My extended family

3

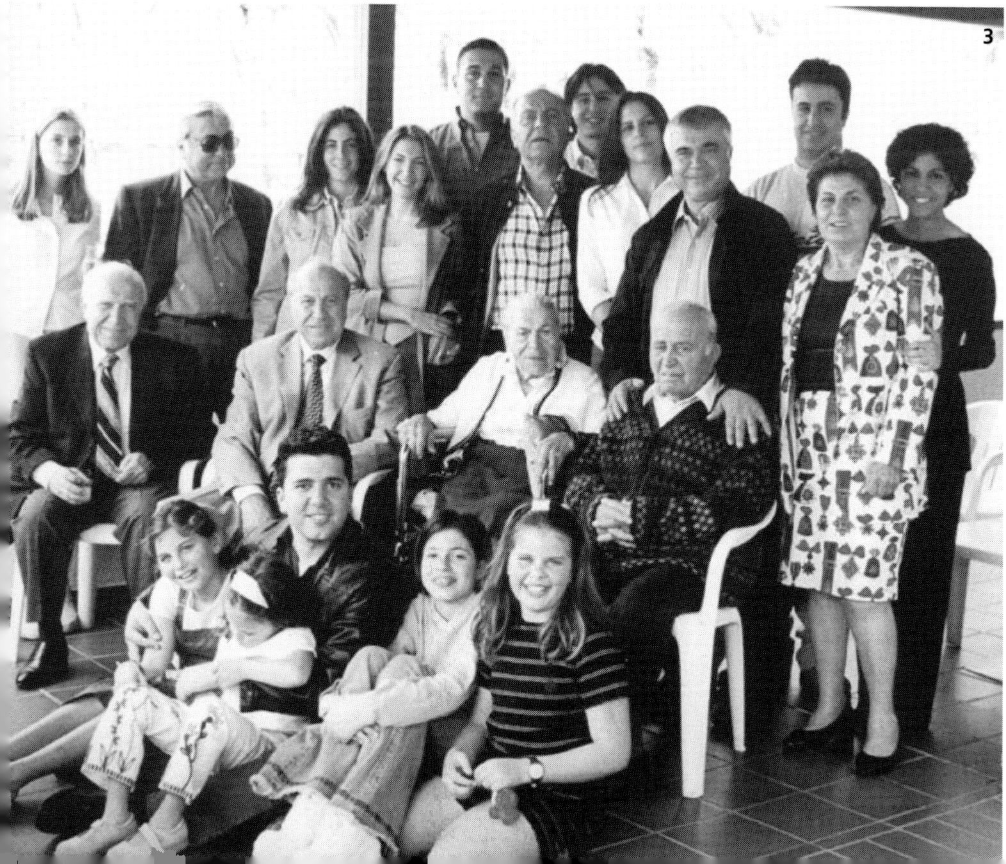

Memories of Childhood

4 During my high-school days, at Assi River, Homs
5 With my cousin Khalil at Tripoli High School (1950)
6 With a classmate, Robert Karam, on the beach in Tripoli (1950)
7 With classmates on a visit to Damascus (1949)

University

8 My graduation day from AUB, with my brother Antoine – June 1957. My grandfather is on my left, surrounded by relatives from our village.

9 With my father and classmates from the Engineering School, on the roof of our house in Dedde

10 (*standing, left to right*) My cousins, Michael Hanna and Samir Zakhem, my brother Abdallah and myself. (*seated, left to right*) My cousin, Khalil Zakhem, and my brother Antoine

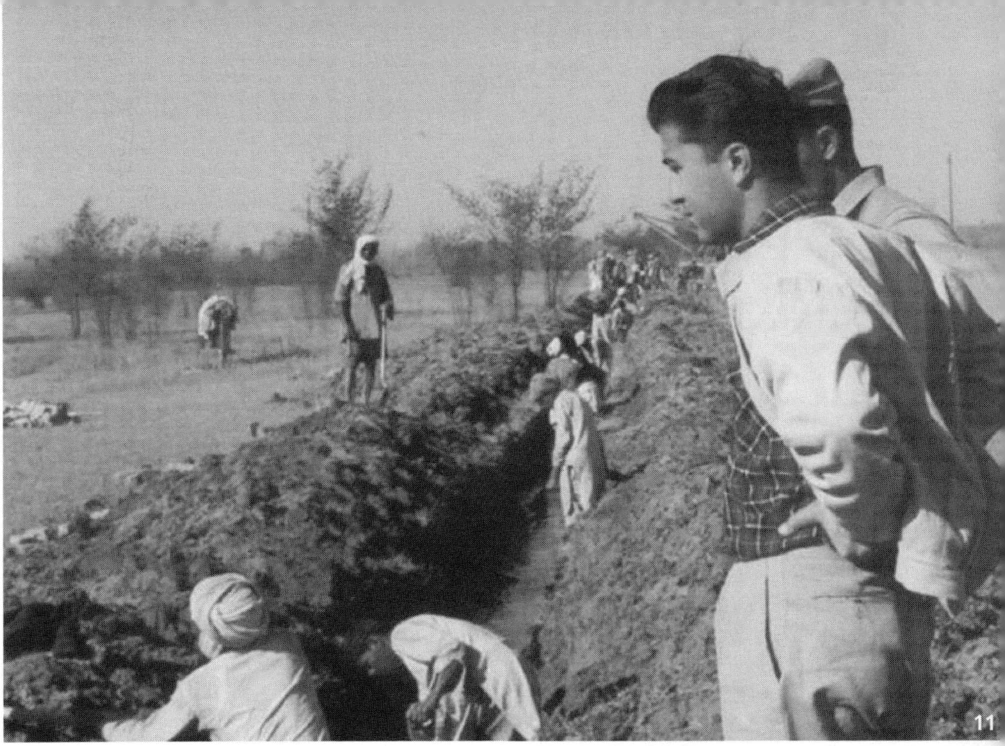

11

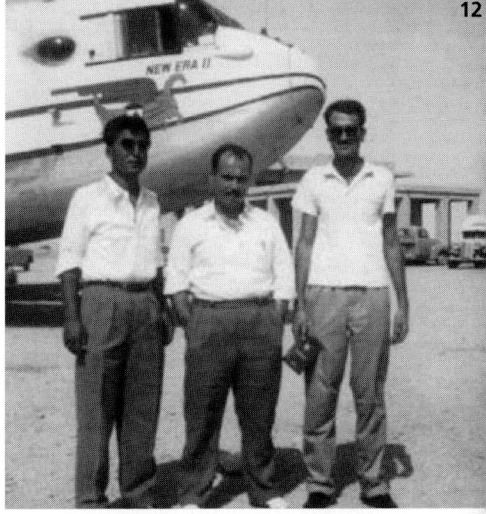

Working in Pakistan

11 At a job site in Kahrian in1958
12 Just before boarding the DC4 in September 1955 to fly back to Beirut, with Emile Jeha on my left
13 With my friend, Zaki Shammas, in 1959
14 With Michael Zakhem in Qatar – 1955

12

13

14

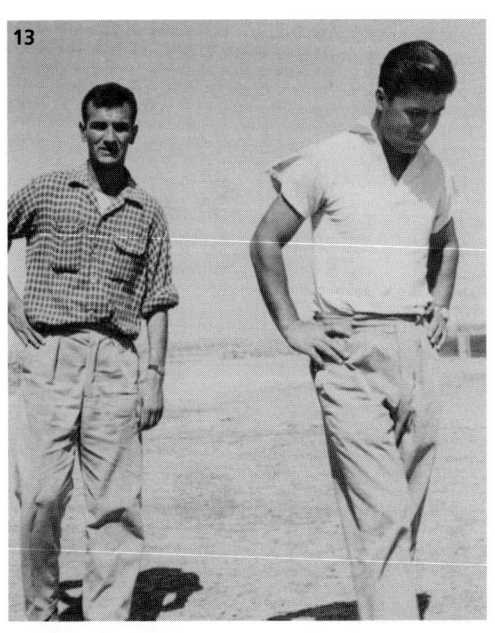

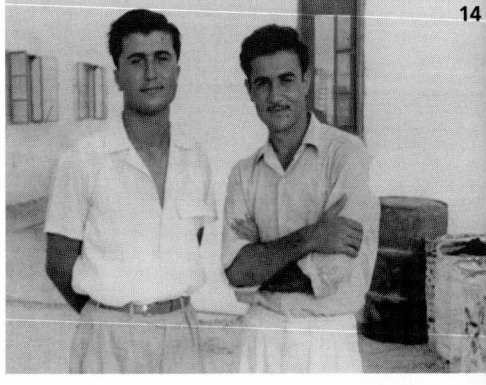

15 With Emile Bustani (*second from right*) in Pashawar, surrounded by some of the CAT employees and with Salim Nassar (*second from left*) and Radwan Mawlawi (*on Emile's left*)

16 With Emile Bustani and a friend at a party in Karachi, sponsored by Emile to honour Prime Minister Karami in 1963
17 Shaking hands with President Nasser, at Lahore Airport – 1959

18 With Bassim Azzam (*left*) and Marwan Khartabil (*right*) in Multan, Pakistan – 1960
19 With Marwan Khartabil at the Yaldizlar restaurant, Beirut, in 1962
20 The farewell reception in my honour, before leaving the Kahrian project and moving to Multan. Wad Ghabriel is on my left.

21 On my wedding day, November 14th 1969
22 My wife, Lisa, and I in London – 1985
23 With my sons, Salim and Marwan, in Monte Carlo – 1987
24 With my son, Marwan, and my brothers: Antoine, Abdallah, Ibrahim and Albert
25 With my wife and children in our London home – 1985

26 Salim and Fay on their wedding day
27 My two sons, Salim and Marwan
28 With my granddaughter, Chloe, in 2008

we had finished the first set of houses; all units in the colony were completed and occupied by the end of April 1963. By the beginning of November 1963, we had started work on the second and third colonies, located at Chuhurkana and Katchaku. I remember that I was at the Chuhurkana site when I heard the news of President John F. Kennedy's assassination on the BBC World Service.

For me, housing construction was a new field of activity, and I had to learn a great deal. The greatest challenge we faced was to use the most primitive methods to produce a product of high standard and at high speed. We manufactured approximately 100,000 bricks and tiles a day moulded from clay and baked in a kiln under the surface of the ground utilising coal as fuel. The clay had to be selected from local borrow pits, then mixed with water to a suitable proportion to become paste-like. Men prepared the clay and women placed it in the steel tile and brick moulds. After one hour, the steel moulds would be ready for re-use and the moulded tiles and bricks left in the sun for a day to dry before being placed in the kiln. Kiln work is an art that requires experienced workers. Kilns are arranged in the form of closed rectangular channels around one foot below the surface. Coal fire is fed at one end and flows inside the channels to the other end seeking its way through the chimney stack, which stands fourteen metres high. The baking process takes around thirty hours, depending on the size of the kiln. One knows the process is complete when the smoke emerging from the stack turns from black to white. Then, the earth is removed from the surface and the baked bricks and tiles are removed and stacked in batches of 2,000. We classified bricks and separated them by quality, including deformed, over-burnt, under-burnt, standard, and first class.

We conducted durability tests on the bricks in the laboratory of our consulting engineers, Tipton & Kalmbank. Bricks classified as standard in size, colour, and strength were used for external walls. Deformed bricks that had the required strength were used on internal walls that were to be covered in plaster. To provide the work site with 40,000 standard bricks and tiles per day, we had to construct three kilns and operate them in sequence. On average, we employed fifty bricklayers, and I can vouch that the best and most efficient bricklayers in the world are Pakistanis, followed closely by Indians.

Due to the rapid progress achieved on this project, TALIHAP enhanced its reputation in the industry. As a result, our company negotiated two other contracts with two different clients working for the Water and Power Development Authority on the Indus Basin Scheme. Although Vihari was my base, I visited Karachi and Peshawar at least once a month to oversee the business of CAT and Mothercat, as well as to supervise other projects. Progress on the Peshawar project was well in hand under the able supervision of engineer Nadim Majzoub.

We maintained an area office in Karachi to provide assistance for ongoing projects and to develop future projects. A major job came our way for the construction of the first Atomic Centre in Rawalpindi. We formed a consortium with an American company and Motherwell. Our company was responsible for the facility's civil works. Our competitor on this bid was another American company with Macdonald Layton as local civil contractor. Negotiations were conducted with the Atomic Energy Commission acting as the client on behalf of the Pakistani Ministry of Power and Mineral Resources, presided over by Minister Zulfaqar Ali Bhutto.

Although our bid on the civil works was approximately 30 per cent lower than that of our competitor, our Chairman, Emile Bustani insisted that we should pursue this project. When I was questioned by Emile on the progress of negotiation on this commission, I informed him of the likelihood that we may lose despite the fact that our bid was the lowest. One hour after leaving his office, Emile's secretary, Mrs Jardack, forwarded a copy of a letter Emile sent to President Ayoub Khan. In it, Emile explained the position of the CAT consortium in this project and complained about the process of negotiation being carried out with the Atomic Commission. Emile went on to stress the fact that our bid would save the government of Pakistan a substantial amount of money – 40,000,000 rupees – about $4,500,000 at the time. He then informed the President about the forthcoming visit of Rachid Karami, the Lebanese Prime Minister, to Pakistan, and his plans to accompany the Prime Minister so that he could discuss the subject further with him or the Atomic Energy Commission. The President acted promptly and arranged for Emile to meet the Minister of Power and Energy directly on his arrival to Karachi.

Rachid Karami was a distinguished Sunni Muslim political leader who hailed from one of the most respected families of Tripoli. He entered the political arena in 1951 and, from 1955, he intermittently served as Prime Minister of Lebanon for eight terms. In 1987, he died in a helicopter crash which is widely believed to have been a deliberate act of sabotage.

Other opportunities came our way. In September 1962, we were invited by the US Corps of Engineers to bid on a project in Saigon, Vietnam. I passed the information to Emile Bustani in Beirut. His reply was swift; he declined the work because he said that Vietnam was headed for a major civil war. Instead, Emile wanted to focus our efforts in Pakistan and the Indian subcontinent. He was right; shortly thereafter, war broke out in Vietnam.

* * *

Throughout this busy period I continued to correspond with my friend Marwan Khartabil. He had graduated in September 1962 with a Master's degree in Structural Engineering from Cornell University. He wanted to return to Beirut to resume working with CAT in an area of his preference. His wish was to be assigned to any project for which I was responsible. He came back to Beirut for the New Year, where he planned to discuss his future posting with our company's management.

I myself arrived in Beirut from Karachi around December 20th. I was met at the airport by Marwan who had arrived a week earlier. During our stay in Beirut, I took him to visit my home village of Deddeh. He expressed admiration for the people of my village and was struck by their sincerity and openness. In fact, two families in the village named their new-born sons, Marwan, after him.

Marwan was a Palestinian who had two brothers and one sister. His father, Adeeb, who was a medical doctor, and his mother, Wadia, moved with their children from northern Palestine to Lebanon in 1948 in the midst of the Arab-Israeli war. Having lost everything they had in Palestine, Marwan's parents had to build a home from scratch and give their children the best education they possibly could. Some of their efforts were dedicated to serving the Palestinian people and their cause.

Wadia was the Founding President of the Union of Palestinian Women, an organisation she started in the early 1950s. Adeeb served on various committees dedicated to defending the right of the Palestinians to a free and independent country. Marwan, for his part, grew up in an atmosphere of family love coupled with national service. He was intelligent, joyful, considerate, and politically engaged. He received a Loan-in-Aid from CAT to study in Britain. He graduated with a Bachelor's degree in Civil Engineering and joined CAT. He was posted to work on my project in Pakistan, and after one year he enrolled at Cornell University for his Master's degree.

During his senior year at Cornell University he was elected President of the Arab Student Union in the United States. This reflected his political ambition and made it possible for him to meet and exchange opinions with Arab ambassadors at the United Nations and other diplomats. At all times he served the cause of the Palestinian people with dignity and common sense.

* * *

Emile Bustani was a close friend of the Khartabil family, a friendship that went back to the 1930s when Emile set up his CAT company in Palestine. Relations between the two families strengthened after the Khartabils had to leave Palestine and come to live in Beirut as a result of the 1948 war. In the 1940s, Emile Bustani's CAT company had branches first in Aden and Iraq, then Kuwait, and after that the Trucial States. By 1950, CAT had become the leading construction company in the Arab world and in the greater Middle East. Emile was a man with ambition coupled with great vision. He predicted the future importance of the Middle East due to the region's oil and mineral reserves. In 1956, CAT moved into their new headquarters, a seven-storey building in Beirut. Emile's offices occupied a major section of the sixth floor, from which he conducted his company's business, a business with interests extending from Nigeria in West Africa, to North Africa, to the Middle East, and to Pakistan.

As a Lebanese, Emile Bustani was an Arab nationalist who was devoted to the Arab cause in Palestine and defended the right of the Palestinian people to an independent country. As a graduate of the American University of Beirut, Emile admired the democracies of the Western world and befriended many of its politicians, especially members of the British Parliament and of the United States Congress. Nevertheless, he was critical of Western governments and their policies regarding the Palestinian issue, but his criticism of the Soviet Union regarding this same issue was far more disparaging and severe.

Because Emile was fervent about politics, he decided to enter the Lebanese political arena, winning election to Parliament in 1952. His campaign style was a true reflection of his personality and worldview. Emile engaged voters on a personal level, listened to their concerns, and proposed sensible solutions. He also demonstrated that he was a modern man who knew how to use technology to connect with the electorate. For example, he was one of the first Lebanese politicians to distribute campaign leaflets by means of dropping them from an aeroplane flying over his constituency. In this way, his message reached even the remotest hilltop villages. Once in office, Emile was a leader who resisted all efforts to convince him to align himself with a narrow group or political or religious faction. Most notably, he was a prominent reformist and an eloquent foe of sectarianism, the political disease that to this day infects the Lebanese body politic. By the early 1960s, Emile was poised to become President of the Republic of Lebanon.

Emile believed that wealthy Arab countries should share a small portion of their tremendous wealth with the poorer states of the Arab world so that the former could improve the latter's social and economic conditions. In his book, *Doubts and Dynamite*, Emile proposed that the Arab oil producing countries donate 5 per cent of their oil income to a newly established Arab Development Fund modelled on the World Bank and operating under the auspices of the Arab League. Donations from Western oil companies that conducted business in the Arab world would also be solicited. In this way, Arab countries that were less fortunate and in need could borrow from the Fund under favourable terms to develop their resources and infrastructure. Although the Lebanese government eventually endorsed this proposal, ultimately and sadly, it was not adopted. The initiative, however, was one manifestation of Emile's long-standing commitment to pan-Arab political and economic cooperation. In fact, perhaps even more than the presidency of Lebanon, he aspired to be General Secretary of the Arab League. I remember well his remarks about the Arab League. He thought that it embodied the great ideal of Arab unity, but it had failed badly in implementing the policies to achieve that unity.

Although he decried the failures of some Arab governments and institutions, Emile had exceptional confidence in the ability of the rising generation of young Arabs to bring about much needed change. He believed that, if given the opportunity, the young generation of every country would be able to achieve standards equal to those prevailing in the most developed nations of the world. His own company, CAT, was an example proving his theory. In the span of only fifteen years, CAT had achieved a reputation comparable to any major European or American company operating in the Middle East. The company was, in fact, a training ground for young Arab engineers and technicians where they acquired knowledge about the construction industry. CAT gave them an opportunity to build confidence in themselves as professionals who could face any challenge. Emile carefully maintained a personal relationship with all of his employees and followed their careers with great interest.

By 1962, I felt that I, too, had established a special relationship with Emile. I knew he was pleased with my performance while working for his company. I noticed also that Emile admired Marwan Khartabil. He saw Marwan grow and develop, and followed his studies at Loughborough University and then at Cornell. He also monitored Marwan's performance when Marwan worked with me in Pakistan.

During my two-week Christmas vacation in 1962, I met with Emile every other day in his office to discuss our work in Pakistan, and to follow up on matters that needed our attention. On several occasions I asked Emile to post Marwan to Pakistan under my supervision. Every time I posed the question he would look sideways through the window towards the sea and say, 'George, forget Marwan. I've got other plans for him.' Marwan invariably asked me about my conversations with Emile, and I told him what Emile had said: 'He wants you here. He has other plans for you.'

The first day of work in January 1963, I left the office with Marwan to have lunch. As the door of the lift opened on the ground level in the reception area, we spotted Emile standing on the sidewalk in front of the entrance waiting for his car. A few senior managers stood around him, including Chief Engineer Adel Dreik. Emile was looking out with his back to the entrance door chatting with the crowd around him.

The Beginings of an Independent Professional Career in Lebanon

Marwan said, 'Look, I don't want to go out and join the crowd so let's wait here until they leave.'

I replied, 'I can't do that, Marwan. Better we go back to the office and come down in five minutes.'

As the lift door started to open, I heard Emile calling, 'George, come back here.'

I looked behind me and there was Emile entering the reception area through the main door. He approached me and took Marwan by the hand saying: 'Marwan is not going with you to Pakistan. He's staying with me here. I have a special plan for him, is that clear? You have your brother Abdallah with you; that should be enough for the moment.' I could tell Marwan was furious but he remained silent.

The next day, Emile called me to his office to say he would be visiting Pakistan on January 23rd with the Prime Minister of Lebanon, His Excellency Rachid Karami. He said to me, 'I want you to go back to Karachi and organise the programme of the visit in co-ordination with the Lebanese embassy.' I was told that the Prime Minister was to visit Pakistan upon completion of a visit to India. The Pakistani Minister of Foreign Affairs, Ali Bogra, had requested the visit by our Prime Minister and was scheduled to welcome him at Karachi airport. Emile also wanted to greet the Prime Minister on his arrival at the airport and then to officially join his delegation in his capacity as member of the Lebanese Parliament.

I returned to Karachi on January 7th and contacted my friend Dr George Dib, Lebanon's Chargé d'Affaires in Pakistan. We agreed to co-ordinate our efforts in preparation for the up-coming visit. The Prime Minister was scheduled to arrive at Karachi airport from Bombay around 5:00 p.m. on January 24th, but one day earlier, the Foreign Minister of Pakistan, Ali Bogra, died of a heart attack at Dacca airport. Emile Bustani learned the news in Beirut while boarding a KLM flight on the evening of the 23rd. Ambassador Nadim Dimeshkiya and the Chief Editor of the *Assafa* daily newspaper, Salim Nassar, accompanied Emile. Dr Dib and I had our doubts whether the visit of our Prime Minister would take place following the death of Foreign Minister Bogra. Pakistani President Ayoub Khan cleared away any doubts by issuing an order appointing Zulfaqar Ali Bhutto as Acting Foreign Minister. Bhutto was ordered to oversee all aspects of the Prime Minister's visit. We were relieved by this news, and from that moment everything went as planned.

For the first time, I was exposed to a high-level political environment and witnessed the conduct of senior politicians, including the Lebanese Prime Minister and his delegation. It was a great experience to meet and talk with senior figures from Lebanon as well as their Pakistani counterparts. I attended official banquets, press conferences, social gatherings, and private dinners. I also travelled with the Prime Minister's delegation on the presidential aeroplane to Rawalpindi and Peshawar. In each location the Regional Governor and his senior officials hosted us. Because it was Ramadan, we observed the fast until sunset and directly afterwards we had a light meal breaking the fast, *Iftar*, followed by an official dinner held at approximately 9:00 p.m.

My greatest satisfaction, and indeed joy, was to be in the company of Emile Bustani. At the end of his ten-day visit to Pakistan, Emile had left an indelible impression on my mind, and my respect for him had increased enormously. I saw him as a successful and ingenious founder and Chairman of CAT, an astute politician, and a dedicated and honourable member of the Lebanese Parliament. I discovered in him those special qualities that make a great leader and distinguish him from others. As a human being, Emile was both compassionate and caring. As a business and political leader, he was energetic, compelling, intelligent, and of great integrity. The memories of those days are so alive in my mind that I am struck to this day by the many ways that Emile, the man, embodied the best traits of Lebanon, his country. I remember that nineteenth century sense of industriousness combined with a twentieth century appreciation for technology. I remember also the sensible Lebanese patriotism enriched by a rational pan-Arab nationalism, as well as that commitment to building economic and cultural bridges between the East and the West, and the deep reverence for the achievements of both the Christian and the Islamic civilisations.

When Emile arrived at Karachi Metropole Hotel it was around 6:00 a.m., and so he suggested that we all have breakfast before going to have some rest. While chatting at the breakfast table, he enquired about the location of the future CAT building. I said it was approximately a ten-minute walk from where we were. He then said, 'I've brought the drawings as prepared by the famous architect

The Beginings of an Independent Professional Career in Lebanon

Edward Stone from New York, so let's walk to the site and show my friends what our headquarters in this country will look like.' We all walked to the site, and on the way Emile kept talking about the company and its future expansion. We stopped on the sidewalk of the major street bordering the site and Emile held the drawing of the master plan in his hands and started explaining to his guests the quality and the beauty of the future building. Then he addressed Ambassador Nadim Dimeshkiya and said, 'Look, Nadim, just imagine that in two years time the CAT flag will be flying over the top of this building at this important spot.' He was totally committed to the growth of the company and wanted it to achieve an international reputation comparable to that of Bechtel and Wimpy. As I have mentioned, Emile was convinced that the new generation of Lebanese and Arabs, if properly guided, would attain great success in every field of human endeavour.

On the day of Emile's arrival in Pakistan, he and I visited the Lebanese embassy and then went to the Ambassador's residence. Emile asked Dr George Dib about his absent wife, Lola. George apologised on her behalf, explaining that she was expecting and confined to bed by her doctor.

George said, 'She is very sorry and rather upset at being unable to see and welcome you to her home in Karachi.'

'I do understand,' replied Emile, 'but can we visit her?'

'Of course,' George said, 'she will be thrilled to see you.'

We went straight to her bedroom and she said, 'Welcome, Mr Bustani, I'm sorry I cannot leave my bed.'

He interrupted, saying 'I shall sit next to you and give you some fatherly advice.'

He held her hand and said, 'To have a baby is the best and most important thing that will happen to you and George in your married life. Please don't forget that. Don't take any chances and be sure to obey the orders of your doctor without hesitation.'

He showed total concern for her, telephoned her a few times during his visit, and asked George Dib about her condition on a daily basis.

Business and politics are invariably mixed, particularly in developing countries. Emile discovered this fact as early as 1951 which encouraged him to enter the political arena by taking a seat in Parliament in 1952. From that date, he refused to allow his company to do any work with the Lebanese government. In this way, he avoided conflicts of interest. Instead, CAT focused its activities in other countries of the Middle East and Africa.

In the early 1960s, Emile was among very few Maronite parliamentarians who were designated as aspirants to the presidency in 1964. However, the chairmanship of CAT took priority, and he would not abandon the company for the sake of the presidency. In 1961, to safeguard the interests of the company, Emile proposed to his two partners, Shukri Hanna Shammas and Abdallah Khoury, to transform it into a PLC (public limited company) by distributing 49 per cent of its shares to the senior and junior staff. The new shareholders would select an Executive Board to run the company, thus relieving Emile of direct responsibility as CEO. Abdallah Khoury objected to this proposal, but Emile did not give up and continued to discuss the idea.

During his visit to Pakistan, Emile exemplified the ideal Lebanese politician and the experienced international businessman. As a member of the official delegation, he was disciplined and highly respectful of the Prime Minister. Whether at public functions or in private meetings with members of the delegation, Emile addressed the Prime Minister at all times as 'Your Excellency'. Two incidents that occurred on the first and second days of the visit are worth recounting. After the Prime Minister arrived at the VIP guest lounge at Karachi airport, a press conference was held. The Pakistani press kept asking about Kashmir and enquiring about Lebanon's stand on that volatile and sensitive issue. Knowing the background of the issue and having just completed a visit to India, the Prime Minister said that the matter was now being discussed at the United Nations. He added that Lebanon hoped for an amicable and peaceful solution. This response, diplomatic in the extreme, obviously did not satisfy the reporters, one of whom asked: 'Mr Prime Minister, we are a Muslim country and we have always supported the Arab cause of the Palestinian people, and we shall continue to do so. We know that you want to maintain good relations with India and we do appreciate the official stand of your government on this subject, but what about your personal opinion? We are curious to know!'

Emile was sitting next to me and when he heard this leading question posed, he jumped up from his chair and said, 'Gentlemen, gentlemen. You are being unfair to pose this question to His

The Beginings of an Independent Professional Career in Lebanon

Excellency in this manner. His Excellency cannot divorce his opinion from that of his government, and anything that His Excellency says will be construed as the opinion of his government. Consider me, for instance. I'm an MP and there are ninety-nine MPs like me in Lebanon's Parliament. I can assure you that we all believe in the rightful cause of Pakistan in Kashmir.' No further questions on this subject were asked, but more were posed about commercial relations between the two countries. The Prime Minister pointed his finger at Emile and said: 'This is the man who will answer your questions.' Emile then explained how the commercial relations between Lebanon and Pakistan were growing in various fields, and that CAT was setting up a partnership with the Pakistani industrialist, Adamji Group, to build a jute factory in Nigeria. The press conference ended and the Prime Minister expressed his gratitude for Emile's timely intervention.

On the second day after his arrival in Karachi, the Prime Minister and his delegation visited President Ayoub Khan at his office in the Presidential Palace. Later that day, I went to Emile's suite at the Metropole Hotel and, as I was passing through the lobby, I read the Reuters press release of the visit. When I entered his room, Emile was in a jovial mood talking to Ambassador Dimeshkiya who was sitting on the couch next to him.

He said to me, 'George, what news do we have from Beirut and other areas?'

I started to respond by saying, 'Please, let me first read this press release. It says, "President Ayoub Khan received the Prime Minister of Lebanon, Rachid Karami, and his delegation at 10:00 this morning. Emile Bustani, MP and a member of the delegation, presented to the President a copy of the Quran which was some 500 years old and handwritten in gold ink."'

On hearing this, Emile seemed somewhat uneasy with the way this news was reported. He asked me to call Salim Nassar immediately. When he spoke to Salim, he told him: 'I have asked you not to print my name in any news report for as long as the Prime Minister is in this country. Please change the Reuters release which you have drafted to read as follows: 'Emile Bustani presented, on behalf of the Prime Minister of Lebanon Rachid Karami . . . ' Emile was so careful about protocol, and he was not in any way prepared to overshadow the Prime Minister of his country. The subtle difference between the earlier Reuters report, and the second one which Emile had suggested indicated his loyalty to his country and his integrity to diplomatic propriety.

Shortly after the newspaper incident, Emile and I found ourselves sitting together as we awaited the next event on the official schedule.

Emile said to me, 'George, you have received a special "salam" from a good friend of yours, Zaki Shammas. He's now married, as you probably know. He's been given the job of constructing the Beach Hotel project in Abu Dhabi.'

Nadim Dimeshkiya, who was also present, said to Emile, 'You surprise me every time I see you. With all the problems you have on your mind, how can you possibly remember the name of one of your engineers in Abu Dhabi or that he is a friend of another engineer working for you here in Karachi? It's really amazing.'

Emile responded, 'The company is only as good as the people who work in it and to appreciate that is half the battle of ensuring the continued success of the company. That's why it's important not only to know who is working for you, but to take an interest in their well-being. Yes, a company needs sound management but it also needs a workforce that is content and also appreciated.' With this explanation, Nadim remained silent.

Emile then stood up and started pacing the room, saying, 'Look Nadim, you know that I'm a contender for the presidency of Lebanon, which is due next year. You know I have all the chances to succeed because the Arabs as led by Egypt are on my side. The British have for a long time been on my side. The Americans are now on my side and the French are finally coming round to my side. There is nothing holding me back from becoming the next President of Lebanon, except the chairmanship of CAT, and this I've just now resolved. For the past two years I've been trying to convince my partner Abdallah to release 49 per cent of the shares of the company to the employees so that I'm assured of its continuity, but he would not agree. Today I have a telex from him agreeing to 25 per cent instead of 49 per cent, and I shall agree. Therefore, the road ahead of me is clear and I hope to succeed. I have great plans for Lebanon, and I pray to God to give me the opportunity to realise them.'

As a witness to all this, I saw Emile's sterling qualities shine. It was precisely this decisiveness, vision, and pragmatism that had enabled him to succeed in business, politics, and the no less risky sphere of philanthropy. Moreover, he had attained success in all his endeavours while also achieving the seemingly impossible: he was widely popular in Lebanon and the Middle East but also highly respected in Western political and business circles.

Emile Bustani was a man of action *par excellence*, and he exemplified his ability to act in two instances. The first instance was in February 1955 when Lebanon was hit by a severe earthquake that demolished over 200 villages in the mountains. Emile was appointed as Minister of Public Works and he took it upon himself to rebuild those villages in the shortest possible time. He created an independent Reconstruction Authority to rebuild damaged houses within six months, and he succeeded in achieving this goal.

The second instance was when Britain and France, assisted by Israel, waged a war against Egypt in 1956 to liberate the Suez Canal. The second day of the invasion, Emile was appointed as an unofficial envoy on behalf of Egypt and entrusted with a special mission. He immediately flew to London to lobby Westminster to bring an end to all hostilities in the Canal zone. As soon as he arrived in London on a chartered private aircraft, he began at once making his contacts with key personalities in Britain. He consulted with his friends in the House of Commons and distributed to every Member a small pamphlet about the war on Egyptian land, suggesting that the war should stop, not for the sake of Egypt but also to protect British interests in the Middle East. The same day, the two great powers, the US and the USSR, issued stern warnings to the invading countries to stop the war and withdraw their troops. The following day the war ended; Emile's mission was a success. In response to the following question posed by the eminent and respected Egyptian journalist Mustafa Amin: 'President Nasser extends his regards and would like to know what he can do to reward you for what you have done.' Emile replied, 'Please send my regards, admiration and respect to the President. I am ready to sacrifice all I have for the sake of the Arab cause but I also plead with President Nasser and the Egyptian government not to make any public announcement as to my role in bringing about an end to this conflict for as long as I am alive.' It was not until 1964, a year after Emile Bustani's death, that his role was revealed to the public by Mustafa Amin.

The following day I flew with the Prime Minister and his delegation to Peshawar, the capital of Pakistan's Northern Province, aboard President Khan's private aeroplane. After a three-hour flight we arrived at Peshawar airport, where the Governor of West Pakistan, Amir Mohammad Khan, Nawab of Kalabagh and other dignitaries were waiting to greet us. The governor was an impressive figure in his white *sirwal* and *kamis* with a white-ribboned turban. The Northern Province is the land of the Patans, known as the land of the Khan family, or sect. They speak their own language, Pashtu, which is quite different from Urdu. Also, their physical appearance and general character are more akin to Afghanis than to their fellow Pakistanis.

The city of Peshawar sits high above sea level and is surrounded by mountains that extend all the way to Pakistan's borders with Afghanistan and Kashmir and close to the legendary Khyber Pass. In those days, a large American airbase was located close to the city. On its grounds CAT was constructing a sewage treatment plant which was to serve 100,000 people. We had around five expatriates from Lebanon working on this job, which was about halfway completed at the time of our visit. Emile found the time to visit the site with me and was pleased with the work. In fact, the sewage treatment plant impressed him so much that he asked me to send him a detailed report on it as soon as possible. He wanted this report because he was developing a ski resort at Dahr Al Bayder in the mountains of Lebanon, called Al Bustan, and intended to install a similar facility there.

The next day we visited the campus of the University of Peshawar, where the Chancellor bestowed an honorary doctorate on the Prime Minister. Afterwards, a special function took place at the university's assembly hall attended by all faculty members along with dignitaries and students. The usual speeches were then exchanged between the Chancellor and the Prime Minister. The remainder of the day was spent touring certain important locales, including the city bazaar and the famous Peshawar Club.

During our stay in Peshawar, the CAT company organised a special *Iftar* dinner in honour of the Prime Minister. The dinner was held at the company Guest House which had been transformed into an elegant hall with a rich banquet of Lebanese dishes. Emile Bustani and I were there and received the Prime Minister on his arrival. Moved by the elegance of the room and the melodious voice of Fairouz playing in the background, the Prime Minister said to Emile: 'Emile Beik, you amaze me. I feel that I am in Lebanon. We are so proud of you and of what you have achieved.' Emile answered, 'Your Excellency, Lebanon is wherever we are, and wherever we are, Lebanon is.'

After our visit to Peshawar, we took a flight to Rawalpindi, our final stop in West Pakistan. The Prime Minister and his delegation were taken to Government House, but I thought Emile should stay at the Fleshman Hotel because it afforded greater comfort and better facilities. About one hour after we checked into his suite and started to go over the correspondence of the company that was copied to him from all areas, I heard a knock at the door and went to open it. I was surprised to see the Prime Minister's Chief of Protocol standing at the door. He was invited to come in, and as he stepped in he said: 'His Excellency the Prime Minister would like to pay Mr Bustani a visit.' Then in walked the Prime Minister himself.

Emile welcomed him, saying, 'Welcome, Your Excellency. What a great honour this is.'

The Prime Minister replied, 'When I settled into my quarters at the government guest house, I asked about you. I was surprised to hear that you weren't with us and that you decided to stay at this hotel. Then I decided to visit you to make sure that you're all right and comfortable. Now that I'm here, however, I can see you've taken the right decision.'

Emile replied, 'Thank you, Your Excellency, you're being very kind and I do appreciate your concern.'

Because it was Ramadan, no tea or other refreshments were offered to the Prime Minister, who stayed to chat for about ten minutes and then left us to do our work.

In the evening an *Iftar* dinner was held at 6:30 p.m. in George Talia's home. It was attended by around 150 guests and was given in honour of the Prime Minister and his delegation. Ministers and high-ranking army officers were among the guests, which included the General Manager of Attock Oil Company and senior members of his staff. The evening was long and tiring, and at around 10:00 p.m. I slipped out with a couple of friends to go to the Fleshman Hotel nightclub to relax and enjoy a change of atmosphere. Before leaving the dinner, I told Salim Nassar not to mention anything to Emile. I told Salim: 'Just say I was tired and had to leave.' Half an hour later, as I was on the dance floor with a lady friend, she whispered in my ear, 'Look who just entered the club.' I turned around to see Emile puffing on a long cigar, watching us with a big smile on his face. I stopped dancing immediately and asked him to join us at our table. He said, 'I'll have one drink.' He ordered a brandy, chatted with us for a few minutes, and then excused himself, saying 'Enjoy yourselves and I'll see you in the morning.'

The next day we met with the Chairman of the Pakistan Atomic Energy Commission, Dr Osman, to discuss the atomic energy tender that CAT's consortium had submitted to the Pakistani government a few months before. This meeting was arranged by Zulfaqar Ali Bhutto, Pakistan's Minister of Power and Energy, and it had been preceded by a meeting with the Minister that had taken place in Karachi.

After the meeting with Dr Osman, Emile sensed that our position was not strong and would require additional reinforcement to be successful. I hinted to him that because our price was low and atomic plants were a new field of construction, it might be advisable to allow this job to slip by, thereby potentially avoiding large financial losses. Emile looked me in the eye and said, 'Listen, George, the loss doesn't worry me. We need to build an atomic power plant. It's very important for the company.' I responded, 'OK, Mr Bustani, obviously you know better.' That same day, Emile decided to end his visit to Pakistan early and return to Beirut. It was nearing the end of January 1963, and he was scheduled to make a long visit to West Africa and the United States in February. Shortly after Emile left Pakistan, the Lebanese Prime Minister's visit to the country also ended.

During Emile's last night in Pakistan, we sat in our hotel discussing many issues, both business and personal. At one point, he asked me when I was going to get married. In the course of our conversation, it was decided that I should return to Beirut in June and take a management post at the head office. This arrangement would also give me an opportunity to find a wife. The next day, as he said farewell to me, Emile embraced me and said, 'I've become so accustomed to having you around during this visit. I'm going to miss you. Hurry up and come to Beirut in June; I shall be waiting.'

The Beginings of an Independent Professional Career in Lebanon

I had no way of knowing it, but these parting words would be the last I heard from Emile Bustani.

After Emile's departure from Pakistan, I immediately went to work on the report he had asked for on Peshawar's sewage treatment plant. I mailed the document to him in early February. A month went by and I did not receive any correspondence from him, which was unusual. I was on the lookout for a letter or a telegram from Emile and became increasingly disappointed that none arrived. A feeling of anxiety persisted until the night of March 15th 1963, when I saw Emile in a dream, a dream that went something like this:

> I arrived on an unannounced visit from Karachi to Beirut to spend a long weekend. On the way from Beirut airport to my house at Hamra I spotted Emile at the Jordanian embassy dressed in black top hat and tails. He was pacing the salon of the embassy that overlooked the main road from the airport on one side and the blue Mediterranean Sea on the other. I tried to pass without being seen. As he turned to walk towards the sea with his back to the road, he changed direction halfway, saw me and shouted: 'What are you doing here?' I replied, 'It's my brother's wedding and I'm going to attend.' He said, 'How come I'm not invited? Can you tell me?' I replied, 'Well, Mr Bustani, it's in fact not really a wedding but an engagement.' He realised that I was making it all up but he accepted it with a smile. All of a sudden the scene changed and I was in the living room with him and saw a painter standing on a ladder, applying a coat of whitewash to the ceiling. In doing so he was splashing drops of white paint on Emile's top hat and tails. I pointed this out to Emile and suggested that he move in order to avoid being splashed. He looked at me and said, 'They are doing a good painting job . . . don't you think so?' 'Yes,' I said. He then asked, 'Are you able to produce the same quality at Vihari?' 'Even better,' I answered.

And then I woke up from the dream. In the morning I was happy because I had seen Emile in my dream and I had a feeling that a letter from him would arrive that day. When I entered the mess hall to have breakfast, our accountant, Yaccoub Bufarah, noticed the happiness on my face and said, 'It's good I see you smiling very early this morning. There must be some good news.' I told him I saw Emile in my dream. Alas, my happiness did not last for more than an hour. On arrival at my office, a telegram was handed to me. It read:

> Company plane crashed on 14/03/63 Beirut shore with Chairman on board stop hopes of survival are remote stop rescue efforts continue and we will keep you informed stop please keep to your work as usual stop A. Khoury and S. Shammas

Devastated by this news, I called together my senior staff, namely Wadie Ghabriel, Abdallah Zakhem, and Yaccoub Bufarah, and read them the telegram; shocked by the news we had just received, I read the telegram several times out loud.

We had no way of telephoning Beirut and so our only source of information was the BBC World News. We listened to it and obtained the story in full. Emile was on his way to Amman for an Arab Bank meeting. Also on board were Dr Nimir Toukan and my best friend, Marwan Khartabil. The pilot was John Ogilvi, the same pilot as on my flight to Kahrian in 1959. Late in the afternoon, the authorities announced that Emile was confirmed dead, but there was no news about the fate of the others on the aeroplane. I was devastated and felt that a part of me was lost and gone forever. My thoughts were overshadowed by the memories of the days I spent with Emile and Marwan during the last Christmas and New Year holiday. I was anxious to learn whether Marwan had survived or not, and spent most of the evening and a few hours into the night trying to get through to Beirut by telephone, but without success.

When I finally went to sleep, I saw Emile again in another dream. He was relaxed, sitting on a couch wearing a jacket and loosened tie. He looked at me with a soft smile and said, 'Put your mind at rest. I've taken Marwan with me.' I woke up feeling miserable, sad, and confused. Emile was my hero and Marwan was my self-image: full of life and vigour. How could I lose both in such a tragic accident? It was utterly unbelievable. I reflected on the days that I spent with both of them in Beirut and Pakistan, and was depressed. I felt that my dreams for the future were shattered. To this day that incident remains the greatest shock I have ever experienced.

In April 1963, I received a letter from Adel Dreik, Chief Engineer of CAT, telling me that prior to his death Emile had assigned me to a management job at Beirut headquarters. Adel invited me to come to Beirut in June to take over as Project Manager of the

The Beginings of an Independent Professional Career in Lebanon

Tripoli refinery project. I went to Beirut and met with Shukri Shammas and Abdallah Khoury to discuss the company's operations in Pakistan and my future. As a result of this meeting, I concluded that I could not carry on working with CAT and decided to liquidate the partnership and launch my own business. Shukri Shammas agreed to this proposal, and steps were taken to dissolve our partnership. I informed Adel Dreik of my decision and thanked him for his assistance. He understood my position and wished me the best of luck. At the same time, I communicated with my brother Abdallah in Pakistan and we agreed that he would join me in starting a new company. I returned to Pakistan for a short visit to finish my work there.

The year 1963, then, witnessed the end of one phase of my life and the beginning of another.

By early 1964, our company – Zakhem Engineers – was formed and registered in Beirut with offices in the Edison building on Bliss Street.

CHAPTER 6

The Founding of Zakhem Engineers

Having liquidated my partnership with CAT I formed a new company with my brother Abdallah. In 1964 our new limited liability company, Zakhem Engineers, was founded in Beirut. Wadie Ghabriel held a small share but then sold it back to us in 1969. The objectives, according to the by-laws governing its operation, were namely to undertake civil and mechanical engineering and construction projects in Lebanon and elsewhere. Immediately after establishing our headquarters, I secured relatively small contracts for two jobs with the Ministry of Electricity in Lebanon. Although delighted with my company's first two contracts, I was nevertheless determined to obtain other projects both in Lebanon and abroad. The first opportunity came when I read an official announcement in an English newspaper about a public tender for an aviation hydrant system at Baghdad International Airport. I immediately wrote to the consulting engineer, Sir Alexander Gibb and Partners, expressing interest in submitting a tender for the job. To my surprise we were accepted on account of my experience in similar projects over the past seven years. We submitted the tender in my name in August 1964, and by December we had secured the contract. This, of course, was the best Christmas present I could have received.

During the first week of January 1965, I travelled to London with our agent in Iraq, Ihsan Rifaat, to sign the contract at the offices of Sir Alexander Gibb and Partners. My brother Abdallah took charge of the project in Baghdad. I negotiated with Shukri Shammas in Beirut to take over CAT's equipment yard and stores located at Kazthmiyya, Baghdad. In only a matter of days, then, we were well established and began work without any significant problems or delays. All the materials for the job were purchased through our Beirut office from approved suppliers in the United Kingdom. As the project moved forward, our client – Iraq's

The Founding of Zakhem Engineers

Directorate of Roads and Bridges – expressed satisfaction with the progress. In order to monitor and maintain the progress of construction, I made monthly inspection visits to Baghdad. At the same time, I was on the lookout for additional work. An opportunity arose when I met the owners of a Libyan contracting company, Al I'mar. They were searching for a sub-contractor to perform mechanical, electrical, and equipment installation for a 100-bed hospital at Tarhuna, Libya. After some negotiation, our company was chosen as the sub-contractor, and we opened an office in Tripoli in mid-1965.

Although both Iraq and Libya are rich in oil and gas, the two countries share few other similarities. Yet the two countries needed to improve their infrastructure, and so Zakhem Engineers was fortunate to expand its operation in both countries by taking other contracts. Of course Iraq, with a population eight times that of Libya, offered more and better opportunities. Furthermore, oil had been discovered in Iraq as early as the 1930s and the country was politically more mature, having secured independence more than twenty years earlier.

During the early 1930s a consortium of major international oil companies such as BP, Shell, and Mobil formed the Iraq Petroleum Company (IPC). IPC was given an exclusive concession to extract and market Iraqi petroleum (for its part, Libya began granting oil concessions to foreign companies in the mid-1950s). Under its agreement with the Iraqi government, IPC was obliged to contribute a portion of its profits to various infrastructure projects in Iraq. The Iraqi government also created a Development and Construction Board that was funded from oil revenue. In this way, Iraq's oil revenue financed a construction boom which benefited many contracting companies, both Iraqi and foreign. CAT, for example, obtained so many contracts that one of its partners, Shukri Shammas, took up residence in Baghdad to oversee its Iraqi operations. He remained there until the early 1960s, when he was forced to leave by the military ruler Abdulkarim Kassim, who had seized power in a coup in 1958.

During Kassim's coup, Iraq's King Faisal II, along with members of the royal family and Prime Minister Nouri Al-Assaed, were summarily executed. Another army officer, Abdul Assalam Aref, staged a coup in 1963 and in turn removed Kassim. Aref died in a helicopter crash while flying between Baghdad and Basra, and his brother, Abdul Raham, assumed power. In July 1968 General Ahmad Hassan Al Bakre, supported by Ba'ath Party leaders including Saddam Hussein, staged yet another coup. Al Bakre was sworn in as President with Saddam as his Vice President. Saddam became the regime's leading figure in the mid-1970s. For his part, Saddam remained as President of Iraq until March 2003 when, as the world knows, the United States and its coalition partners launched a war against Iraq and removed him from power.

I knew Iraqi students during my high school and university years in Tripoli and Beirut and had befriended a few of them. I admired what I had seen of Baghdad during my short visit to that city in 1956. The people of the city were welcoming and the town itself was orderly and well developed in comparison with Beirut. My ambition to work in Iraq was fulfilled when my company was granted the aviation fuel hydrant project at Baghdad International Airport.

In addition to the airport project, and within a few months of entering Iraq, Zakhem Engineers established itself as a highly acclaimed contractor in the oil and gas industries. In fact, we were short-listed as qualified contractors and approved by Iraq's Directorate of Oil and Planning and Construction Administration (OPCA). In 1965, we secured a contract to lay an oil pipeline 75 kilometres long from Tikrit to Samarrah. Shortly after, we were selected by SPIE (Société Parisienne Pour l'Industrie Electrique) to construct the Kirkuk-Baghdad twin gas pipelines, each 300 kilometres long.

In late 1966, SNAM (a division of ENI) came to Baghdad to build a new Luboil plant at the Daura refinery. They sub-contracted to us the tank farm which comprised of constructing seventy-two tanks of different capacities. Having done well on that work, SNAM retained us for other projects around the world, including two refinery projects in Sri Lanka and the Bahamas.

In 1967, Zakhem Engineers formed a joint venture with the NKK Corporation of Japan to construct a water line in Iraq. The project entailed pumping water from the Mandali River in eastern Iraq to towns up to 100 kilometres away through a 56-inch pipeline. In spite of fierce competition from French, Italian, and German companies, we succeeded and obtained the letter of intent for the project at the end of May 1967. Sadly the Arab-Israeli war of 1967 prevented the execution of the project. Less than three years after its launch, Zakhem Engineers had gained such an excellent reputation that in subsequent years we were able to obtain major contracts in the oil sectors of the Gulf States. In 1966, for example, we began to construct an oil depot for Amin Oil Co. in Ahmadi, Kuwait.

As Zakhem Engineers expanded its operations, I gained experience in the financial side of the business which was new to me because I did not perform such work during my time at CAT. Now, a considerable part of my time was spent negotiating with banks for project financing. To obtain a credit line, we had to demonstrate a steady cash flow into the company. In the construction industry, tender bonds, performance bonds, and advance payment guarantees – all in the form of bank guarantees – are basic features of any project.

As our business developed, I found myself shouldering a great responsibility to reach agreements with various international banks. Especially challenging was arranging financing in a country into which Zakhem Engineers had just moved. In a new country, one does not yet enjoy a reputation with local banks and businesses. In order to secure agreements with banks on a specific contract, we had to provide collateral guarantees and an assignment of revenues from the client to the bank on the project. In addition, we also had to provide our own personal guarantees. Now versed in the financial side of construction, I realised just how risky a business this was. So much came down to reputation and trust; thus, on-site performance remains the very essence of the industry.

As Chairman of Zakhem Engineers, I was also responsible for public relations. Like finance, this was a time consuming activity and involved extensive international travel to introduce the company to prospective clients. Through 1965, my travels were restricted to the Middle East and Europe. In 1966, however, I made my first trip to Tokyo to meet with NKK and Chiyoda. Zakhem Engineers and these two companies hoped to form a consortium to bid jointly on the Za'afaraniya project in Iraq. This was my first trip to the Far East, and I stopped over for two days in Hong Kong on my return trip to Beirut.

I was fascinated and impressed by what I saw in both Tokyo and Hong Kong, but I also remember how frightened I was when the aeroplane approached Hong Kong airport for landing. The aircraft skimmed above towering apartment blocks before touching down on a runway built on reclaimed land surrounded by the deep water of the ocean. Hong Kong is a densely populated city, and what struck me most about the place was the heat and also the hustle and bustle of the city. By contrast, Tokyo seemed like an orderly town, very clean and calm. The people of Tokyo are highly sophisticated and they take pride in demonstrating this quality to visitors. I spent three days at the NKK offices and one day at those of Chiyoda. I met with teams of Japanese engineers and senior managers as we worked to draft the tender for the project.

Usually, after working for long hours, I was invited to dine in famous restaurants and nightclubs on Ginza Street. I was introduced to geishas and for the first time I tasted Kobe beef. As a result of my visit, I concluded – as others had warned me – that negotiations with Japanese companies are both difficult and tedious. My Japanese counterparts insisted on going into much greater detail than we did in the Middle East. Each meeting was devoted to a single engineering subject like civil, electrical, mechanical, instrumentation, or testing. During every negotiating session I met with a team of engineers and had to answer a long series of questions. All questions and answers were recorded and circulated to all participants on the same day.

After I returned from my trip, we submitted our consortium's offer to Iraq's OPCA. Alas, the job did not materialise and I realised that all our time, effort, and money had been wasted. I also realised that this process might be repeated at great expense to our company.

By 1967, having established our reputation, Zakhem Engineers began receiving many enquiries from multinational companies aspiring to do business in the Middle East. My brother Abdallah and I had a basic understanding whereby he, as President, supervised operations and I, as Chairman, managed the development of the business. At this time my main concern was to achieve growth for the company. I spent most of my time meeting with potential new clients, including oil companies and government ministries and agencies. The process of obtaining a specific project can take months, and at any given time we were pursuing as many as four tenders simultaneously. With so much going on, the business occupied all my time.

The Founding of Zakhem Engineers

Late in 1967, we were informed about a major project in Abu Dhabi. The government there intended to build a 14-inch pipeline to transport gas from the oilfields at Shames to a new power plant on Abu Dhabi Island. The length of the line was to be 130 kilometres, and the project also entailed construction of a dehydration plant at Shames and a desulphuring plant at Almaqtaa, (um-annar) Abu Dhabi. This construction was the first major project of its kind to be launched by the newly oil rich Emirate, and many international companies were keen to participate. Zakhem Engineers was interested in doing at least some of the work, but for technical and financial reasons we were not capable of taking on a project of this scale on our own.

Quite unexpectedly we were contacted by a company based in Milan, Italy, called Snamina, a joint venture between SNAM of Italy and INA of Yugoslavia. Snamina proposed forming a consortium whereby they would provide project management and material procurement, while we would perform the actual construction. We soon agreed on terms, and our consortium submitted the tender in February 1968. Our price was the lowest and, after strenuous negotiations, a contract was signed in the summer of the same year. In the course of preparing the tender, I made a few trips to Milan with our estimator to meet and work with Snamina's team. This visit to Milan gave me an opportunity to learn more about the Italian people, including their character and business habits. Through close observation, I noticed that there are certain similarities between the Lebanese and the Italians.

After work on the Abu Dhabi project began in earnest, the name Zakhem Engineers became well known in the Gulf region. Except for motor vehicles, most of our construction equipment was mobilised from our resources in Iraq. We built a base camp in Abu Dhabi. In addition, we purchased an established sub-camp from the Olayan company which was located around 80 kilometres from our base camp at Za'afaraniya.

At that time, Abu Dhabi was hardly visible on the map. It was practically a barren land except for an oasis, two beach-front hotels, and the White Palace (the official residence of the country's Emir, Sheikh Zayed bin Sultan Al Nahyan). An industrial area was allocated to those companies that were involved in construction and other services. The seaport was insignificant and featured just one jetty. The airport was still under construction. Before the airport was opened to commercial traffic, airlines flew to the RAF airport at Sharjah. From there, it was necessary for our personnel to travel overland in four-wheel drive vehicles. This trip took approximately three hours, depending on the condition of the road which was made of compacted sand, sprayed with heavy oil on the surface. On occasion, sections of the road were flooded by sea water during high tide and became impassable.

Sheikh Zayed launched a major construction and development plan that brought tremendous changes in only a few years. Abu Dhabi itself was raised almost two metres using earth transported from special borrow pits on the mainland. This prevented flooding during high tide. Roads, highways, and other basic infrastructure, including water distribution systems and sewers, were constructed. Power generation and desalination plants were established. In fact, our gas pipeline project was destined to supply gas to the first power plant in the country.

*   *   *

After my return from Pakistan in 1963, I lived with my parents in Beirut in a flat on Leon Street. Traditionally, Lebanese men and women lived with their parents until they married. Two of my brothers, Abdallah and Ibrahim, were abroad, which meant that there were three brothers and three sisters living with my parents. The eight of us shared a four-bedroom flat, a situation that made for fairly uncomfortable living. Despite the lack of space, there were advantages to living at home. My mother was an excellent cook and, like most mothers, loved watching others enjoy her food. My mother was so adept at serving large meals that our friends joked how 'Zakhem's restaurant' was open for lunch from noon to 3:00 p.m.

A constant subject of discussion, both at home and in social gatherings, was when to get married and to whom. Many friends and family members were keen to introduce me to girls whom they considered suitable to be my wife. I was in no hurry to marry because I was engrossed in my work and totally committed to the success of our company. However, after my brother Antoine was married in early 1967, extra pressure was placed on me to follow suit. I started giving the prospect of marriage serious thought and met a few girls on pre-arranged dates but nothing serious developed, and I let it be known that I would not be rushed into marriage. My sister Georgette, however, had other plans and in the presence of my mother said to me, 'George, I just want you to meet this one girl.' The young lady in question had visited our house twice, my mother liked her, and she was a college classmate of my sister. Her character and background were beyond reproach and she was beautiful. I told my sister to arrange a meeting.

A few days later, in early December 1967, I received a message from my sister to come home as soon as possible. I was having coffee with some friends at the Horseshoe Café at Hamra, but I made my apologies and left to go home. When I arrived, my sister introduced me to Lisa Masad with whom I had a pleasant conversation for about fifteen minutes. Lisa was a woman of exceptional beauty with long black hair that reached her waist, and that beauty has never faded to this very day. She spoke good English, French, and of course Arabic. Lisa was born in Alexandria, Egypt, where her father ran the family business. She was educated in Cairo until June 1967 when her studies were disrupted by the Arab-Israeli war and she had to move from the American University of Cairo to the Beirut College for Women.

From our conversation, it was obvious to me that Lisa did not realise that my sister had carefully planned our 'chance' meeting. Afterwards, I asked my sister to arrange other social interactions with Lisa. Lisa and I saw each other one more time before I departed for London, where I had already made plans to spend the Christmas and New Year holiday with my friend Camille Bustani. While in London I stayed at the Londonderry (Metropolitan) Hotel on the corner of Hyde Park. Although the visit to London was a pleasant break from my work, Lisa was always on my mind. I called my sister and asked her to invite Lisa to spend New Year's Eve with us. If she accepted, I would return to Beirut and join them for the occasion. Lisa agreed, and I immediately left London in time to celebrate the New Year at the Printania Hotel located in one of the most beautiful spots in the mountains of Lebanon.

During a New Year's Eve party, while dancing with Lisa, I whispered in her ear that I was highly impressed by her character, beauty, and charm and that I wanted to marry her. She was stunned at my proposal and said she did not know whether to answer yes or no. She said, 'You know, I still have a year and a half before I graduate from college. I need some time to think before I give you my answer.' Lisa's words made me respect and appreciate her more then ever. I told her to take all the time she needed but I hoped in the end she would agree to my proposal.

On the first day of the New Year I visited Lisa's home and I was introduced to her family: her parents, her two sisters, and her only brother. They were gracious, hospitable, warm, and kind, and so I naturally felt comfortable around them. Lisa's father, Nicolas Masad, was an experienced businessman and impressed me as a highly cultured, wise, and knowledgeable gentleman. He was a Lebanese from Zahlé who had emigrated in the 1920s to Egypt where he and his brothers had built sizeable industries in Cairo. By the late 1930s, Nicolas Masad was a wealthy man. He was married to Rose Kadri, a girl from his native town of Zahlé. Lisa was the youngest of their children.

The Masad businesses took a turn for the worse after the Egyptian revolution of 1952. By 1961 all foreign businesses in Egypt were nationalised, and Lisa's father was stripped of his assets. His only compensation was his appointment as an administrator to run the former business he owned at a nominal salary. In June 1967, after the onset of the Arab-Israeli war, Nicolas moved his family to Beirut. There, Lisa enrolled in the Beirut College for Women while her brother and two sisters worked to support the family. Lisa's father was only sixty-seven years old, but in a short period of time he had aged beyond his years and looked like a man of seventy-five. He was quiet and calm and spoke in a soft manner without ever losing his temper. He had developed a heart problem and high blood pressure and was on medication. He never liked to discuss his former businesses in Egypt. Whenever Lisa or any other member of the family said something about their past life, he would interrupt them and say, 'What's wrong with our life here? Thank God we are happy and in good health!' He was a man who had written off his past and was now trying to help his family to build a new life. He knew, however, that his physical ailments and financial difficulties were real and a cause for great concern.

Over the following two months I met with Lisa often so that we could become better acquainted. We never went out alone but always in the company of relatives and friends as was the custom at the time. By the end of February 1968, Lisa accepted my marriage proposal and we were formally engaged around Easter. The biggest hurdle for us was the difference in our ages: I was twelve years older than her. Most of Lisa's girlfriends of the same age group felt that this age gap was not acceptable. Her family, however, thought otherwise and they were very supportive of our union. After our engagement, we started going out alone and as time passed, I discovered how deeply I cared for her. We finally made plans to get married immediately after her graduation in June 1969.

* * *

Between 1967 to June 1968, in the midst of my search for a wife and later during the time of working out marriage plans, our company landed three major contracts that increased our workload threefold. The first contract was in Iraq, where we were awarded construction of a government Social Security building, the second largest in the centre of Baghdad. The second contract was for gas pipelines in Abu Dhabi, and the third was for the construction of an oil refinery tank farm in Colombo, Sri Lanka.

To fulfil these contracts, we had to launch operations in two new countries, a significant challenge. My brother Abdallah was heavily engaged in our work in Iraq, so I had to oversee the new projects by shuttling between Beirut, Abu Dhabi, and Colombo. I appointed my trusted friend Wadie Ghabriel as our Area Manager in Abu Dhabi; his brother, Asaad, filled the same role in Colombo. My brother Ibrahim had by this time begun to work for our company as a Trainee Engineer on a project building two oil storage tanks in Kuwait.

The flights I took from Beirut to Colombo were routed through Karachi and Bombay. On my first visit I did not feel at all like a stranger thanks to certain similarities between Sri Lanka and Pakistan, where I had lived and worked for over six years. My experience in Pakistan helped me a great deal when launching our operation in Colombo. Since both countries were under British rule, they essentially had the same system of government. In those days there were few five-star hotels in Colombo, a beautiful city with white sandy beaches on one side and tea plantations on the other. I chose to stay at the Galface Hotel where I was told that a team of actors, producers, and directors had stayed while filming the famous movie *The Bridge on the River Kwai*.

Our company's Ceylon project entailed building fifty-two steel oil storage tanks of varying sizes. We recruited our technical staff, including a contingent of welders and fitters, from Beirut. We brought in construction equipment from our stocks in Iraq and Kuwait. It was fairly easy to find accommodation for our expatriates in private houses located near the refinery site. Work on this job went smoothly and our client was satisfied.

Unlike Colombo, mobilisation in Abu Dhabi was very difficult. We had to provide accommodation for our crew by building our own camps and sub-camps on land allocated by the government for the duration of the contract. We also had to construct our central office. Abu Dhabi had nothing to offer and all food supplies, materials, and consumables had to be imported from Kuwait or Beirut. Water for domestic use was brought from Bahrain and we produced our own electricity on diesel generators. Knowing beforehand what challenges we would face, we started to reduce our volume of work in Iraq so that my brother Abdallah could spare some time to assist us in Abu Dhabi.

As noted previously, in July 1968 a group of former army officers and senior members of the Ba'ath party staged a coup d'état in Iraq. Opposition politicians were killed en masse. Our company did not emerge from this political turmoil unscathed. We had approximately 400 people working on four different projects in the country. The political instability, naturally, caused economic unrest, and we faced demands from our workers to pay higher wages. On top of this, other factors like transport costs increased significantly. Our workers increased the pressure on us by threatening to go on strike with the support of the Iraqi Ministry of Labour. At this time, labour ministry officials as well as officers of the Iraqi tax bureau made frequent visits to our headquarters in Iraq, where they demanded all manner of information.

Under severe conditions, my brother Abdallah struggled to maintain our operations in Iraq. In early April 1969, Abdallah was scheduled to join me in Abu Dhabi. He did not arrive as planned, and instead I received a telex from my brother Ibrahim (in Beirut) telling me that Abdallah would arrive in a couple of days. I was highly sceptical of this information because it came from Ibrahim instead of directly from Abdallah.

The Founding of Zakhem Engineers

The day after receiving Ibrahim's message, I received a telephone call from our company's lawyer in Baghdad, Kazim Hamdan. He told me that he had arrived in Abu Dhabi and was staying at the Beach Hotel. Fearing something was terribly wrong, I asked him to come to my office immediately. Upon arriving, Kazim Hamdan said to me, 'George, listen to me carefully. Abdallah was arrested by the Iraqi internal security police one hour before leaving for the airport to take a flight to Abu Dhabi. You know how confused the situation is now in Iraq under this new regime. Therefore, you must act fast and secure his release. Abdallah has not yet been charged with a crime, but you can never tell if or when that will happen. Your brother Antoine has already contacted various authorities in Beirut. I have one more thing to say: I cannot act as your lawyer in this matter. Please do not refer to me or mention my name to any contact you have in Iraq.'

Kazim Hamdan's news fell like a bombshell, and for a moment I could not even speak. It took some time after he left my office for me to regain my composure. Having collected my thoughts, I immediately began making plans to save my brother. I informed Wadie Ghabriel and other friends of the news. I also consulted with my brother Antoine and formed a plan of action. We contacted the Lebanese Ministry of Foreign Affairs in Beirut and the Ambassador of Lebanon in Baghdad. These authorities were very sympathetic and immediately initiated contacts through diplomatic channels to obtain Abdallah's release. Meanwhile, I had a scheduled luncheon with my friend Rushdie Al Maalouf, owner and editor-in-chief of the Lebanese daily newspaper *Assafa*. Although I could hardly eat, Rushdie was kind enough to keep me company until it was time for me to leave for the airport.

Because enquiries through diplomatic channels produced no immediate results, we also contacted friends who were members of the Ba'ath Party of Lebanon, namely Dr Abdul Majid al Ra-fii'e, Nicola Firzly, and Jihad Karam. They held discussions with the Iraqi Ambassador in Beirut and also sought an immediate audience with Saddam Hussein himself. Approximately twenty-five days after we first learned of Abdallah's arrest, Jihad Karam travelled to Baghdad and met with high level authorities there. He was also permitted to visit Abdallah in jail. Upon his return to Beirut, he met with our family and told us, 'Don't worry, he'll be freed soon.'

True enough, forty-five days after his arrest, Abdallah was released without charge. My family will forever remain indebted to our friends in Lebanon and elsewhere who did everything possible to secure my brother's release.

This episode had a great bearing on our business in general and my private life in particular. As a result of this imbroglio, I discovered that we had many enemies but few friends. Some who had appeared to be close to us immediately turned their backs at the first sign of trouble. This exposure to the crass side of human nature was both shocking and painful, and I have never forgotten it.

On a business level, we had to act swiftly to regain our momentum, but of course this was not an easy task. First, we had to resolve the existing and pressing problems related to our projects in Iraq. After his return to Beirut, I had a long meeting with Abdallah during which we decided to liquidate our operations in Iraq once our outstanding work was completed. Second, we agreed to intensify our presence in the Gulf States, starting with Abu Dhabi. This meant that Abdallah had to spend additional time in Iraq to sort out outstanding issues and bring ongoing projects to closure. Our Colombo project was going well, but we were experiencing major delays in Abu Dhabi as a result of a dispute with Snamina. Efforts to resolve this disagreement amicably failed, and both sides agreed to an arbitration process in London.

Arbitration was a new experience for me and I had to learn all I needed to know from scratch. Arbitration, a form of alternative dispute resolution, is a technique for the resolution of disputes outside the courts, whereby the parties involved in the dispute refer to one or more persons, the 'Arbitrators', by whose decision they agree to be bound. In other words, it is a settlement technique in which a third party reviews the case and imposes a decision that is legally binding for both sides. As a start, both sides have to sign an agreement which will specify the dispute and confirm their consent to the arbitration process. It took two months of difficult negotiations with the other party before we could reach an agreement that was a clear directive to the Arbitrators. The agreement was signed in August 1969 signalling the start of an arbitration process that took a year to complete.

In the midst of the arbitration process, I received an urgent telex from Milan asking me to visit SNAM's offices to discuss a project at

The Founding of Zakhem Engineers

Freeport in the Bahamas. The next day I took a flight to Milan. On arrival, I was briefed about the job at Freeport and was asked to go there at once to inspect the site and come to terms on a contract.

Upon arriving at Freeport 34 hours later, I was questioned by an immigration officer and asked about the purpose of my visit to which I replied that it was business. The immigration officer refused to grant me entry to the country because I did not have a visa. I said that a visa was not required for a visit of 48 hours or less. He said, 'That's true if you are a tourist, but for business you need to have a visa. No exceptions.' I pleaded with him, but to no avail. The immigration officer contacted an airline official and asked him to have me flown out of the country immediately. My local business contact reported my case to the airport's chief immigration officer, who in turn passed the details to the Governor. Neither, however, countermanded the original decision. I stayed in the airport's transit lounge waiting for my case to be resolved. During this time I met with two engineers from SNAM who were allowed into the transit lounge to talk to me. As I was being briefed on the project and conditions of work in the country, the Airline Station Manager interrupted us saying I had to leave without any further delay. I had been booked on various connecting flights to reach Beirut and I had to board the aeroplane immediately.

I arrived in London the following morning totally exhausted and suffering from a severe headache. I felt I needed some time to recover from the stress of my fruitless trip. I presented my case to the immigration officer and requested a transit visa for two days to rest before taking the next flight. He was kind and understanding and granted me a visa. I flew to Milan after two days and concluded the contract for the project before returning to Beirut.

The whole episode was a painful experience. I had been penalised because the Governor of the Bahamas did not want to hurt the feelings of one his junior subordinates. No one I spoke to in authority seemed to care that I had spent four days crossing three continents to conduct a piece of business that would benefit the Bahamas. I decided to put the sad event behind me by concentrating on the project, which we launched in September 1969.

Amid a great swirl of professional responsibilities, including globe-trotting travels, I was left with little time to attend to my personal life. In fact, for me this has always been the case: my duty to my company takes precedence over everything else. But the fact remained that I was engaged to Lisa and I deeply felt the need to spend more time with her.

Fortunately, Lisa understood my situation and was prepared to wait.

Still, I felt guilty and on one occasion during the summer of 1969 I said to her, 'You know the difficulties I'm going through now, so you're free to change your mind about our marriage if you want.'

She answered, 'George, I didn't get engaged to you because you are rich and wealthy but because of your qualities as a person that I love and admire. I'll be at your side in bad times as well as in good times.'

She went on to say, 'I'm confident that very soon you'll resolve the problems and the situation will improve.'

I was immensely relieved and encouraged by Lisa's reply and felt very proud of her. Suddenly, I realised how understanding and thoughtful she was. To me, she was not a girl of twenty-two but rather a woman of great wisdom and maturity.

Lisa graduated in June with a Bachelor's degree in Political Science from the Beirut College for Women, now known as the Lebanese American University, or LAU. Lisa and I were soon married at the Saydat Al Bishara Orthodox Church at Ashrafiyeh, Beirut, on November 14th 1969.

On our honeymoon we planned to go to Germany for a week to visit Lisa's eldest sister, Nicole, who was married to a German gentleman. Then, we planned to spend another week in London before travelling on to Freeport. We would remain there until the New Year. Air tickets and hotel rooms were reserved according to this schedule. But after spending a week in Germany, we decided to skip our London visit and proceed directly to the Bahamas in order to escape from the cold weather in Europe. I advised our office in Beirut about our change of plans, but alas our plans for a restful vacation in the Bahamas did not come true.

CHAPTER 7

The Challenges of Arbitration and the Blessings of Parenthood

My first business trip with my wife to Freeport in the Bahamas was a journey to remember. It was supposed to be the continuation of our honeymoon after spending one week in Munich. But as we had ongoing projects there it was business mixed with pleasure. Our aeroplane touched down in Freeport around 10:00 p.m. The island was dark and the weather warm and humid. After we had disembarked and entered the arrival lounge to collect our luggage, I looked around to see if anyone from our company had come to the airport to meet us, as I expected and had informed Lisa, but no one was there. Lisa, tired from the long trip, asked me, 'Where are your people and how are we going to get to the hotel? And which hotel are we staying at?' I was at a loss and did not know how to answer her questions. Instead, I went straight to the airport's taxi stand, found a driver, and asked him to take us to the Holiday Inn. At the hotel, the clerk at the reception desk told me that our reservation was for the following week. At that point I realised that our company's headquarters in Beirut had failed to advise our office in Freeport about the change in my travel plans. Fortunately, we were able to secure a room. Lisa was tired and went directly to bed while I stayed awake trying unsuccessfully to contact our resident manager by telephone. Eventually I was able to speak with Assad Najjar, a painting contractor on the project, who was staying at the same hotel.

When Assad saw me he first welcomed us to the Bahamas and then began to explain the extent of the damage on the project. I was taken by surprise and asked him, 'What damage are you referring to?' He said: 'I'm sorry to tell you but I thought you knew that ten days ago a strong storm blew through the refinery site with wind speeds in excess of 225 kilometres per hour. The storm caused extensive material damage. Fortunately, at that time – 4:00 in the morning – there were no people on site, so no injuries occurred. In short, a 45,000 cubic metre tank suffered extensive damage due to the collapse of central columns with roof plates that destroyed all bottom plates and two tiers of the shell plates. A total of 300 tons of steel plates need to be replaced from Italy which obviously will delay the job.' I decided to visit the work site early the next morning to survey the damage and ascertain what needed to be done. I could not sleep at all that night, and I did not want to bother Lisa with the news of the storm so I left at 7:00 in the morning telling her that I needed to visit the work site but would return to the hotel to have lunch with her at noon.

When I arrived at the site, everyone was surprised to see me. I had the opportunity to survey the area in detail and began to relax. In the afternoon, I returned to my hotel at about 3:00. I apologised to Lisa for being late, but we had a wonderful lunch together and then we went to relax by the pool. After some time, I told Lisa about what had happened as a result of the storm that hit the island. She asked, 'Why didn't you tell me this last night?' I replied that I did not want to worry her after such a long trip.

Lisa and I remained in the Bahamas for the next twenty days. During our stay, we made many new friends, notably with the young General Manager of the Royal Bank of Canada, who had just married a woman of Lebanese origin from Antigua. Because my company did business with the Royal Bank of Canada, we developed a friendship based on business interests as well as on personal friendship. The bank manager's mother-in-law was visiting her daughter in the Bahamas. She lived in Antigua, and like all Lebanese emigrants was nostalgic about her homeland. She was especially happy to meet us because it gave her an opportunity to talk in Arabic about her homeland with fellow Lebanese.

In those days Americans would fly to the Bahamas from Miami for weekend get-aways. One of the main attractions for American tourists were the gambling casinos. One evening after dinner Lisa and I went to the gaming room in one of the casinos, but were stopped at the door by the supervisor. He would not allow Lisa to enter because he thought she was underage. We did not have our passports and I, as her husband, explained to him that she was over eighteen and

The Challenges of Arbitration and the Blessings of Parenthood

must be allowed to enter, but he was adamant. I appealed to the establishment's General Manager, who happened to be of Lebanese origin and he eventually allowed us in. This episode was repeated in Miami a week later at the Sheraton Towers Hotel. Sitting in the hotel bar waiting for two friends, the barman refused to serve Lisa because he thought she was underage. This time, because we had our passports with us, we resolved the matter speedily.

I had to return to Freeport for two days before Christmas to attend to certain matters on the job. Lisa preferred to remain in Miami because she was tired of flying. My friends, Dr Mackol and his wife, insisted that Lisa stay with them at their home rather than at a hotel. We agreed to this arrangement, and I flew to Freeport. While in the Bahamas, I called Lisa a few times each day. I sensed that she was lonely and missing me a great deal. Upon my return to Miami, Lisa was waiting at the airport. As we embraced, she started crying and said, 'Don't ever leave me alone again. I'll go with you wherever you want me to go.'

We spent the holidays in Miami, and I remember the time I spent there very well because it coincided with the first manned moon landing. We watched the event live on television. The conversation between President Richard Nixon and the astronauts was a veritable milestone in history.

We returned to Beirut in early January 1970. Lisa and I had much work to do in terms of establishing a household, including furnishing our flat on Sidani Street. Fortunately, my office was only about 100 metres away from my new residence, so I was able to come home for lunch and spend some time with Lisa. Our flat was very close to the American University of Beirut, and we had a beautiful view of the campus and the Mediterranean. I had lived in this area since enrolling in AUB in 1951 and, over the years, had made many friends and acquaintances in the community. This environment, although familiar to me, was relatively new to Lisa.

We remained in Beirut for about one month, trying to settle down and adjust to our life as a married couple. We were kept busy receiving friends and relatives who came to offer congratulations and best wishes for a happy married life. I must admit that we learned a great deal about the joys and disappointments of marriage from the experiences of our married friends.

At that time my brother Abdallah had already moved to Freeport in order to oversee our business in the Bahamas. I was fully engaged in our arbitration process with Snamina regarding the Abu Dhabi project. Meanwhile, we successfully completed our project in Colombo and we were looking for similar jobs elsewhere. Fortunately, our reputation as a reliable contractor was firmly established among the process-engineering firms of the oil industry.

We were asked for the first time to build a tank farm for CTIP (an Italian petrochemical company) at a new refinery project located in Bertonico, near Milan, Italy. I visited Milan in early February 1971 and negotiated the contract with Mario Maraldi, the tank manufacturer. This was the first in a series of jobs we would undertake in Italy, including projects in Pesaro, Sinnetzaro, Sicily, and Trieste. To comply with Italian law we had to establish an Italian subsidiary company, which we called Zakhem Italia s.a.r.l.

After concluding the negotiations in Milan, I left for London to meet with our arbitrator and lawyers, who were acting on our behalf in the arbitration with Snamina. Our team consisted of one arbitrator (Mr Shafik Cotran), one solicitor (Mr Noe Sleigh) and one counsellor (Mr Eugene Cotran). These gentlemen received assistance provided by a quantity surveyor, an estimator, and a construction manager from our staff. The arbitrators were in the process of selecting an umpire in consultation with the Institute of Arbitrators in London. The Institute suggested three potential names and we were asked to choose one.

This was my first experience with arbitration and I had to educate and prepare myself by reading, consulting, and absorbing as much information as possible in a very short period of time. My knowledge on this subject was put to the test on a daily basis. We managed to agree on the name of the umpire with our opponents and the arbitration process began in earnest. After the first arbitration session, two issues were decided. First, the fee for the arbitration was to be paid in advance by means of a joint account to which both sides would contribute equal amounts. Second, both parties agreed to submit a statement of claim within thirty days.

I returned to Beirut to make arrangements for payment of the arbitrator's fee and to draft our statement of claim. Neither item was easy to achieve. My time in the following six months was divided between Beirut, Milan, and London. I also took a trip to Nigeria. Because London was the locale of the arbitration, I rented a furnished flat in the city for use by our staff. Similarly, I rented a flat in Milan that I used during my business trips to Italy. Lisa visited Milan with me on three occasions, and she enjoyed each trip – not least because of the elegance and variety of Milan's shopping centres. Meanwhile, our company's staff and resources were mobilised for the project at the Bertonico refinery, and work began there with minimal delays.

Back in London, the arbitration process proceeded apace. Both sides made submissions, and then each responded to the other side's initial submission and reply. Eventually, our side responded to a series of questions posed by the arbitrators. This took us to the end of April 1970 when the Arbitration Board met and issued their final instruction: the hearing on the case would begin during the first week in June at the courtroom in the Institute of Arbitrators building, London. We were informed that the Institute would charge a specific daily fee for use of the courtroom and for other services. In addition, we had to pay an additional fee to be spent by the Arbitration Board to obtain legal advice. These expenses were to be paid in advance.

I went to London one week before the hearing to meet with our team and consult with our solicitor regarding the hearing procedures. Our company's staff in Beirut and Abu Dhabi had prepared five boxes of relevant documents, including correspondence, photographs, and other supporting materials. Some of our engineers and foremen came in from the field to act as witnesses. Our solicitor and counsellor asked me to deliver the opening statement. They asked me to practise my delivery in advance. The solicitor handed me a copy of the statement and asked me to give him any remarks that I might have. I read and reread the text over several days before presenting it to the Board at the opening session. Abdallah arrived two days before the hearing, which gave us an opportunity to make a general assessment of our position. After consulting our solicitor, we also agreed on the procedure to be adopted during the hearing session.

On the first day of the hearing we assembled in the courtroom of the Institute of Arbitrators where the umpire (Mr Osborne), two other arbitrators (Dr Korompay and Mr Cotran), and two clerks were sitting on a platform. Our team sat on one side of the room and our opponents on the other. The umpire made an opening statement that focused on the rules and regulations of the proceedings. He called upon both parties to signal our approval, which we did. Then I was called to the podium to make the opening statement for our side. My presentation, which lasted about ninety minutes, laid out the problems we faced with Snamina and the damages we had incurred as a result. I was specific regarding the reimbursement we were requesting. In support of the payment we sought, I named a list of six witnesses that could provide proof to the Board of my contentions. Following my presentation, a coffee break was announced, and we adjourned to an adjacent room. During this break, the various members of the opposing teams had come into direct contact with each other for the first time in the eight months since the arbitration process began.

From the conversations that took place during the coffee break, I learned that SNAM had decided to liquidate Snamina, their partnership with INA of Yugoslavia, and take over direct responsibility for this project. SNAM was, in short, reacting to Snamina's poor performance. The arbitration process taking place was, therefore, directly supervised by SNAM. This was good news for our company because our performance on joint projects with SNAM in Iraq, Sri Lanka, and the Bahamas had made us many friends at SNAM.

When formal arbitration resumed, Snamina made their opening statement. Then, the umpire adjourned the meeting until the next day.

In the evening, my brother Abdallah received a telephone call from a friend of his who was employed by SNAM in Milan. Abdallah's contact stated that SNAM wanted to negotiate a settlement to the dispute. If we agreed to this suggestion, Abdallah's friend would fly to London early in the morning to negotiate confidentially with us. In the meantime, arbitration would continue as usual. We agreed to this proposal and the following day Abdallah began negotiating with SNAM while I continued with the arbitration process. Two days later, we concluded a settlement by negotiation and informed the arbitrators. The umpire made a concluding announcement in an official session and the process was declared terminated.

In conclusion, we secured around $500,000, almost 70 per cent of the money we were seeking in arbitration. We considered that

The Challenges of Arbitration and the Blessings of Parenthood

our efforts had been worthwhile. With this sum of money, we were able to pay all our debts on the project and were left with some cash. This experience taught me a valuable and enduring lesson: one should not resort to arbitration but instead attempt to solve all conflicts through direct negotiations with the opposite side. Arbitration, unless forced on you, is a terrible waste of both time and money.

When I flew into Beirut, Lisa met me at the airport and hugged me with tears in her eyes. 'Is there anything wrong?' I asked. 'No,' she replied, 'on the contrary, I'm very happy.' 'Then why are you crying?' 'Because I'm so happy. You are going to be a father.' I held her close, kissed her again, and whispered in her ear that she had brought me great news. I told Lisa that we had to be grateful to God Almighty. As it turned out, her pregnancy was quite normal except for the usual complications during the first three months. As this was our first child, we closely monitored changes in Lisa's physiognomy on a daily basis. I even made sure to buy her maternity dresses from the world-famous shop, Mothercare, on my visits to London.

My involvement in the arbitration process over a six-month period took precedence over everything else, including securing new contracts for our company. I was, therefore, faced with the urgent task of making up for lost time by seeking out new projects. In March of the same year, I made a business trip to Nigeria to study the local market and assess the possibility of establishing a branch of our company there. A Lebanese-Nigerian friend of mine, Yousuf Hammoud, invited me to visit Nigeria and offered his assistance to help me find my way in a totally new environment.

While in Nigeria I visited Lagos, Wari, and Port Harcourt. After weighing all factors, however, I concluded that it would be too difficult for our company to make a start there. During my travels I met Adel Dreik, the Chief Engineer of CAT, who was also visiting Nigeria on business. CAT was heavily involved in road construction projects for the Nigerian Federal Government and other projects on behalf of oil companies. Adel was a good friend and he offered sound advice about working in Nigeria. We left Lagos together on a BOAC flight to Beirut with a stopover in London for two days.

Upon arrival in London I presented my passport to the immigration authorities and requested a transit visa for forty-eight hours. After flipping over the pages of my passport, an immigration officer told me that he was denying my application and that I would have to leave the country on the earliest possible flight. I tried to get him to change his mind, saying that in the past I had always been able to get a forty-eight-hour visa. He interrupted, saying 'I was the one who issued your last entry visa and I warned you not to return without an entry visa to this country, and you agreed.' He then waved to airport security and two Scotland Yard officers escorted me to a van that transported me to a holding facility for illegal aliens.

At the facility, another police officer took charge and led me to a room which was already occupied by a Pakistani citizen. I was told that my flight to Beirut would depart at 10:00 a.m. the following morning and that I should not leave my room until the officer returned to escort me to the aeroplane. That night I could not sleep a wink, but the next morning I boarded a flight out of Britain. This incident was an experience I will never forget.

Having sorted out the problem of arbitration, I was again able to focus on the future. The status of my company was not encouraging. As I have already related, our Iraq operation had been forcibly closed, Abu Dhabi was in the process of liquidation with no jobs in hand or likely to arise in the immediate future, and the Freeport job was on the verge of completion. In short, we were left only with our work in Italy.

*   *   *

Lisa and I had made a habit of spending the summer months in two towns in the mountains of Lebanon. We spent July at the Kadri Hotel in Zahlé and August at the Shalimar Hotel in Baabdat. We liked Zahlé because it is Lisa's hometown and she was pleased to spend time with her relatives and friends. Our first trip to Zahlé as a married couple was a special occasion because all of her family and friends wanted to meet Lisa's husband and to come to know him better. After our stay in Zahlé came to an end, we went to Baabdat for the month of August. My brother Antoine and his wife, Norma, along with two other couples who were close friends of ours, joined us. Being with family and friends helped sustain Lisa during her pregnancy.

Lisa gave birth to our first child on October 24th 1970, at Trad Hospital in Ras Beirut, which was located close to our home. I refrained from being in the delivery room and decided to wait outside with Lisa's mother and my mother. I remember that I looked inside the labour room once at 4:00 a.m. Lisa gave birth at 5:30 a.m. I was ushered into the delivery room by her physician, Dr Ajaj Abulhusun, where I saw Lisa and our first baby. Seeing a new child is a truly unforgettable moment; one is full of pride, happiness, and gratitude coupled with a feeling of satisfaction. I walked out of the delivery room imbued with this feeling and told my mother and Lisa's mother the good news: they had a grandson.

Members of my family and Lisa's family immediately came to the hospital to see the baby and to offer their congratulations. We decided to call him Salim, after my father, who was greatly honoured that our first-born was named after him. Later that day my father took Salim's birth certificate to our home village, Deddeh. He returned two days later and handed me an identity card for Salim that certified his birth in Deddeh on October 27th. When I saw the ID card with this incorrect information, I was furious and told my father to change Salim's birthplace to Beirut. 'No, not at all,' he responded, 'I made it read Deddeh on purpose so that he can vote there, where we all belong.' 'And what about the date of birth as the 27th instead of the 24th?' I asked. 'If you want me to change it, I will; it's very simple,' he replied. But to this day nothing has been changed and, according to his passport, Salim was born at Deddeh on the October 27th and not the 24th at Ras Beirut which is his real birth date and birth place.

Regarding my company's operations, in 1971 we secured a contract along with CMP of France to build a tank farm at Dar es Salaam, Tanzania. Around the same time, we were also asked to submit a bid for construction of a large tank farm for the Azzawiya Refinery in Libya; this contract was eventually awarded to us two years later.

Prospects of obtaining projects in the Arabian Gulf region seemed hopeless when, quite unexpectedly, my friend Michel Malik contacted me in December 1971. He enquired whether we would be interested in building a pipeline in Qatar. I immediately responded that we were indeed interested. Michel then asked me to attend a meeting at the St George Hotel with representatives of the Power Gas Company, who were preparing an offer for an NGL (natural gas liquid) complex to submit to Qatar Petroleum Company (QPC). During the meeting at the St George, I made a lengthy presentation to three representatives from Power Gas including the team leader Norman Stodart. I included full details about our company's history and capabilities. After I finished talking, Norman was impressed and said to me, 'I'm glad we met you. Now we can offer a competitive price instead of that of Faiz Boustany of CAT.' He went on to say, 'We know that you're capable of doing the job, and we know you'll submit a competitive price for the pipeline, but we have to convince Shell in The Hague (the engineers for QPC) to accept.' At the same meeting we agreed on a programme for preparing our bid that would meet the closing deadline of early February 1972. Michel was very supportive and offered the services of his company in Qatar, Orient Contracting, for the ditching of the pipeline's trench.

Although Michel was about seventeen years older than me, we shared similar backgrounds. He came from Bterram, a village in Lebanon's Al Koura district that is located approximately ten kilometres from my own village, Deddeh. After graduating from AUB as a civil engineer, Michel joined CAT during the 1940s and worked there until the mid-1950s, when he left to start Orient Contracting with Elie Zaroubi. Because of our common experiences, Michel and I reached an easy meeting of minds on the Qatar pipeline project. His company specialised in civil works like buildings and roads, and we discussed prospects for a long-term collaboration between our two companies for the purpose of securing oil and gas construction projects in Qatar.

Power Gas Company submitted their offer to Shell in early February. The offer comprised two alternative prices, the first with CAT as sub-contractor for the pipeline and the second with Zakhem as the sub-contractor. The price of the first (with CAT) was higher than the second (with us), and thanks to our lower bid, Power Gas Company would be the lowest among the four tenderers.

During this time, Lisa gave birth to our second boy on February 10th 1972. Once again, we were blessed and thanked God Almighty for another healthy child. This time I made sure that my father registered the right date of birth on the baby's identity card. We named our second son Marwan, in honour of my friend Marwan Khartabil.

Meanwhile, Power Gas Company kept me informed about progress on the Qatar project during the post-tender period. I learned that our file was scrutinised by a Shell team, and they raised many detailed queries. We had to meet their demands, which included furnishing a minute accounting of my work experience beginning with the day I graduated from AUB. I listed all the projects I had executed, including the PRL refinery pipelines project in Karachi for Shell (I listed the name of Shell's Resident Engineer on that project, Mr Goodsy). Two months later, towards the end of May 1972, I received a telephone call from Norman Stodart of Power Gas Company. Norman said, 'George, thanks for giving us the information on your career. We've just finished our meeting with Shell representatives, and they're entirely satisfied with Zakhem. The job is ours! Shell is preparing a letter of intent and they will meet us in Doha soon.' Upon further enquiry, I discovered that the Shell project team referred the files on the project to Goodsy, who then held a senior position in The Hague. Goodsy commended our performance. In fact, he told the Shell project team: 'Rest assured that whatever George Zakhem signs for, he delivers.' It was a pleasant surprise to discover that this man, Goodsy, who some ten years earlier had vetoed my appointment as Project Manager had come forward with such a positive recommendation.

We finally signed a contract with Power Gas Company, and work on the Qatar job began on the first day of August. This was a joint venture with Orient. The project comprised laying a 130-kilometre gas pipeline from Dukhan to Um-Saied. When completed, the pipeline would move gas from the oilfields in Dukhan to the NGL plant at Um-Saied. Faiz Boustany of CAT, our main competitor, was furious when he heard the news that we had been awarded the contract. He contacted Power Gas Company directly after the award and offered a price reduction. When that manoeuvre failed, Faiz reached out to Michel Malik and tried to convince him to break the joint venture between Zakhem and Orient.

At that time, Faiz was President of the Pipeline Contractors Association International division, and he went as far as to tell Michel that he would use his influence to block Michel's access to pipeline equipment. Of course, all of these threats did not succeed and we went ahead with the job as planned. The work was completed in a year, after which Qatar Gas Petroleum Company awarded another pipeline contract to our joint venture. Later on, due to inner friction and disagreements between the partners, Zakhem and Orient went their separate ways. By 1975, we succeeded in obtaining the prized contract for the largest pipeline project in Qatar, namely the Kuff Gas pipelines.

Our business in Italy was progressing smoothly and satisfactorily. During 1972 we were engaged to construct oil storage tanks of 60,000 cubic metres capacity at a Trieste refinery. That same year, we mobilised in preparation for work on the Azzawiya Refinery tank farm in Libya. Amid this good fortune, however, an unexpected event occurred.

In July 1972, an explosion rocked the tank farm at the Trieste refinery. In Beirut, the Popular Front for the Liberation of Palestine (PFLP) declared responsibility for the action. The incident occurred at dawn and a pall of smoke filled the sky all through the morning hours. Police and anti-terrorist squads surrounded the refinery and fire brigades went into action to put out the fire. At 8:00 a.m., our company bus with some thirty welders and fitters arrived at the refinery gate. The police stopped the vehicle and interrogated its passengers, discovering in the process that they were a mix of Lebanese and Palestinians. Without further questioning, the police took our workers to their quarters, confiscated their passports, and deported them to Beirut three days later.

Subsequently, the Italian authorities addressed additional questions to Zakhem Italia s.a.r.l., owned by my brother Abdallah and me. Eventually, we were denied permission to enter Italy. Such a travel ban, besides being personally repugnant in that it implied we were a threat, could ruin our business in Italy. We immediately protested the decision to Lebanon's Foreign Minister. He, in turn, raised the matter with the Italian government at the highest levels, but this demand had no effect. Later, we learned through our lawyers that Italy's Interior Minister had decided that the best way to bolster Italian security was to deny all Arabs the right to reside or work in Italy. Furthermore, this official accused our company of failing to comply with laws governing foreign workers in Italy. In fact, we had submitted the proper paperwork for our workers but it was pending at the time of the Trieste explosion.

A few years after the Trieste incident, the Italian government discovered the identities of the perpetrators, who of course had no connection to Zakhem Italia. But the damage had been done. Our work in Italy was stopped and our company closed its offices in Milan after liquidating our Italian assets. All of the considerable

The Challenges of Arbitration and the Blessings of Parenthood

advantages we would have gained by being established in Italy were denied to us. The Italian debacle was a blow to the company and its potential of doing business not only in Italy, but also in other European countries.

Furthermore, on a personal and business level the Trieste incident continued to reverberate. In 1975, for example, I was faced with the need to travel to Italy on business related to company work on the Homs refinery in Syria. I secured an entry visa from the Italian embassy in Beirut, flew to Italy, and checked into the Principe Savoy Hotel in Milan. I had my meetings during the day and returned to my hotel around 5:00 p.m. About an hour later, I heard a knock on the door, opened it, and found the hotel manager and two policemen standing in the hallway. The manager was apologetic and said to me, 'Mr Zakhem, you're requested to go to the central police station, the Questura di Milano, with these two policemen. My advice to you is to obey their instructions without any objections.' I left my room and walked through the corridors and lobby of the hotel with the two policemen walking beside me and watching me closely. Other hotel guests looked at me with suspicion, as one might expect. I was embarrassed and rather humiliated by this unwanted attention.

Once we arrived at the police station, I sat in the waiting room for two hours before being questioned about my entry into the country. I told the officers questioning me the simple facts: I carried a visa issued by the Italian embassy in Beirut allowing me to visit Italy on business. I told them, 'I've done all that's required, and in a correct manner. There should be no objections to my visit.' Apparently, the police were not convinced and they started making all kinds of telephone calls, which of course I could not follow because they were speaking in Italian. Finally, after six hours at the police station, the officers said that I could go, but that I had to leave Italy within twenty-four hours. Before returning my passport, they made a note of the twenty-four-hour deadline on my entry visa. I returned to my hotel around midnight and left the country in the morning. I did not return to Italy again until 1987. Even those many years later I was worried about how I would be treated by the Italian authorities, so on that occasion I asked my friend Dr Khalil Makkawi, then Lebanon's Ambassador to Italy, for his assistance and he graciously obliged by meeting me at the airport.

Naturally, I was highly disappointed by what I had experienced in Italy, but I never lost faith in our company's ability to achieve success. Our new project in Qatar was critical to the company's future because it could provide the basis for future opportunities in the Gulf States. Around this time I told myself: 'Two years ago (in 1970) after completing arbitration, you aimed to achieve a turnover of $5,000,000 per year. Now you have exceeded this figure with the prospect of a sizeable increase in future years.'

Having taken comfort in our performance over the past six years, despite the setbacks in Iraq and Italy, I was looking to the future with even higher expectations. In 1972, I did a general review of our performance and, based on this study, produced a five-year plan. Our goal was to achieve impressive growth. This meant we had to spend more time on public relations and marketing to promote the company to prospective clients. To this end, we produced our first brochure describing our capabilities. Also, we applied for membership to the international division of the Pipeline Contractors Association (PLCA), which was established in 1966 in Paris. We were admitted as a chartered member of PLCA in October 1972. This was a major step. Then in 1975 I was elected as a member of the PLCA's Board of Directors as the representative for the Middle East and Africa.

At this time, I served for three consecutive years on the PLCA Board, two years as a Director and one year as Second Vice President. During this period, the Board of Directors took three major decisions affecting the entire industry: first, to transform the international division of PLCA (an American Association) to become independent as the International Pipeline Contractors Association (IPLCA); second, to draft the new by-laws; and third, to appoint a new Executive Secretary to replace the present one who was about to retire. I was the youngest member of the PLCA Board, which included myself and twelve other persons, mostly former company Presidents and Directors like Jean Guyot of Entrepose; Paul Simeon of Spie-Batignolles; Filippo Carina of Montubi; Ranald F. M. Grant of Land & Marine; and William Burns of Morrison-Knudsen Int.

The establishment of the IPLCA caused a good deal of controversy. Although its by-laws were accepted by the membership, the decision to locate the IPLCA secretariat in Paris was hotly debated. Some favoured headquarters in London instead. Also, the fact that Board representation was to be distributed by geographical areas also caused a great deal of argument. The proposal was to have ten board members representing ten geographical areas, namely the UK, France, Germany, Benelux, Italy, the Middle East, North Africa, American Overseas, South America, and other areas with two Directors-at-large.

Because the directors-at-large would come from France and Germany, it was obvious that Western European interests would control the Association. If the IPLCA was to be a truly international concern, however, this arrangement was not acceptable. Instead, I proposed the following: that the geographical areas for Western European countries be reduced to three instead of five, that one be added for Eastern Europe (to include Greece and Turkey), and one for Asia (to include Iran). My idea was strongly opposed by some Board members, but to avoid a protracted verbal debate I submitted my proposal in writing to the Association's President and left it at that. I also backed a proposal by the South American Director to hold our conventions every two years in a country outside of Europe. Jean Guyot strongly disagreed with this concept. In short, he acted like an autocrat and was in the habit of reminding everyone of his status as a founding member and President. This was his way of telling us upstarts that his opinion was to be binding at all times.

I believe that everyone appreciated my contributions to the Association. Thanks to my work with IPLCA, the Zakhem firm became recognised internationally as a company of the highest calibre. In 1987, I served on the Board once again and the following year was elected as its President. During my presidency, we held our convention in Singapore. Looking back now, many of the companies that were cornerstones of IPLCA in its early days have long since disappeared, been amalgamated, or are no longer of consequence in the pipeline industry. Yet, to this day our firm is still thriving and becoming stronger than ever.

Unfortunately, construction activity almost came to an end in Lebanon and the Arab world between 1967 and 1973. The so-called Six Day War of 1967 between the Arabs and Israel precipitated this decline, but the demand for construction work began to pick up again in the wake of the October War of 1973. In short, the Zakhem company had to redouble its efforts to achieve the goals it had stipulated in 1972.

CHAPTER 8

Crisis, Success and Honour

During 1973, tensions between the PLO (Palestine Liberation Organisation) and the Lebanese government escalated. In part for this reason, by the summer of 1975, Lebanon was engulfed in a full-scale civil war. In this period of history, the Lebanese people were deeply divided among themselves. Leftist groups supported the PLO, while rightist forces opposed what they saw as PLO interference in Lebanon's internal affairs.

When hostilities broke out in the summer of 1975, I was in Lebanon vacationing with my family at the Shalimar Hotel in Baabdat. The situation was so tense and full of uncertainty that many Lebanese were wondering what would happen to their country. Amid the violence and uncertainty, I brought my family back to Beirut and monitored developments. Shortly thereafter, in September, I left with Lisa to attend the PLCA convention in Acapulco. We decided to visit my brother Albert, who was then studying in Houston for his Engineering degree. A problem arose because we did not have visas to enter the United States, nor could we obtain them from the US embassy in Beirut, which had closed on account of intensified level of hostilities that had spread to the capital and paralysed daily activities everywhere. I turned for assistance to my friend Albert Alexander, who was then Commercial Attaché with the US embassy in Beirut. He saw to it that Lisa and I were interviewed by the proper authorities and issued visas.

Even as Lebanon underwent ominous events that still define the country to this day, the Zakhem company was experiencing a turning point in its operations. First, in 1975 we detached ourselves from Orient Contracting and submitted our first solo bid, to construct the Kuff Gas pipelines for Qatar General Petroleum Company (QGPC). This was the largest contract for which we had ever tendered, and it was valued at 57 million Qatari riyals (excluding pipe supply). We came in below our rivals by a full 10 per cent.

Second, also during 1975, we received a telex from NKK Japan inviting us to bid jointly on a 450-kilometre pipeline from Mombasa to Nairobi in Kenya. We were keen to work with NKK, so we arranged for my brother Abdallah to meet with their team in Nairobi to work out the details of a joint bid.

The major developments in Zakhem's operations that transpired in 1975 came on the heels of a sizeable and prestigious contract that we had secured in 1974. That year, we were selected as the subcontractor for the extension of the Homs refinery in Syria. A company from Czechoslovakia had built the original refinery, but the extension was completed by an Italian company, INGECO. The Homs project was our first contract in the refinery sector, and this gave our company an added advantage in its attempt to secure additional contracts in the field of the construction of oil and gas facilities.

In September 1975, having attended the PLCA in Acapulco, Lisa and I were unable to return to Beirut because the airport was closed due to fighting in the vicinity. We decided to fly to Doha so that I could continue to work on the QGPC tender negotiations. Meanwhile, my mother had moved into our house in Beirut to look after our two children. The hotel we stayed at in Doha, the aptly named Oasis, was full of Lebanese who had fled the civil war in their country. In late October, Middle East Airlines announced that it was about to cancel all flights between Beirut and Doha. On the same day I heard this news, I flew to Beirut and returned the same day with our two sons, Salim and Marwan. In fact, we took the very last flight that left Beirut for Doha.

During that period of rising turmoil and great turbulence in Lebanon, my brother Abdallah handled our joint tender with NKK while I focused on securing the Kuff Gas contract in Qatar. After several revisions in our bid, we received a letter of intent from QGPC on December 30th 1975. This was a truly hectic period because I had spent most of my time during November and December in London trying to establish the Zakhem company's international office in order to replace our Beirut headquarters. We found a suitable temporary office at 100 New Bond Street. My family remained in Doha until the end of November. At that time, we decided that it was best for Lisa and the children to move to Cairo where her parents lived and where we could enrol Salim and Marwan in a suitable school.

As things turned out, business travel and family relocations resulted in me spending New Year's Eve of 1975–6 alone in Doha. This forced solitude gave me an opportunity to reflect on the momentous events of 1975. Even at this early stage, it was clear that the civil war would be a disaster for Lebanon and her people. In addition to the tragedy of lives lost, homes and businesses were being destroyed en masse. Those Lebanese who were able to flee the country and seek refuge elsewhere did not hesitate to do so. In this way, cities throughout the Middle East and Europe – including Amman, Cairo, Damascus, Athens, London, and Paris – suddenly hosted an influx of Lebanese. Many of my fellow countrymen and their families also went to the United States and Canada. It is estimated that over one million Lebanese left the country, a figure which represents 40 per cent of the entire population of Lebanon.

For the Zakhem company, London was a logical new home. By this time, we had concentrated our operations in the Gulf States and in several of the English-speaking countries of Africa, especially Kenya and Tanzania. After extensive consultations with our solicitors and auditors in London, I decided to restructure our group to maximise our options for expansion and growth. First, I travelled to Luxembourg with our legal advisor, Atef Khoury, to form and register the holding company, Zakhem International SA, a task that was completed on December 22nd 1975. The purpose for setting up this company was, and remains, to hold the shares of the entire subsidiary and associated companies operating within our group. Two subsidiaries were essential for our operations in the UK and abroad: Zakhem International Construction Ltd, registered in Jersey CI on January 29th 1976, and Zakhem Construction (UK) Ltd, registered in London on May 21st 1976.

By December 1975, our offices were well established at 100 New Bond Street in London and, henceforth, all correspondence was directed to this address. From London, I was able to communicate easily with Qatar and Kenya by telephone and telex. In addition, daily British Airways flights connected London with both Qatar and Kenya. For personal living quarters I had purchased a three-bedroom flat at Darwin Court, Gloucester Avenue, NW1. With the acquisition of this new property, it was now possible for my family to join me in London.

When I look back at this period, I can see the wisdom of the decisions made by our company to relocate our offices from Beirut to London. Thanks to this move, the war in Lebanon only minimally affected the work of our company in Qatar and Syria. In short, there is no doubt that 1975 was a year that represented a new beginning for our company: a new business plan was drafted, contracts were quadrupled, and Kenya gave us a whole new field of operation.

On January 1st 1976 I flew to Cairo to spend some time with my family, having been away from them during the holidays. Fortunately, Lisa understood the demands of my work. She also appreciated the importance of Zakhem's new projects such as the one in Qatar. During the two months Lisa and I had spent in Doha, she had personally witnessed the tensions and demands of running the company. After spending a few days with my family, I left Cairo for London, where I met with representatives of the engineering company Pencol to finalise details of the Doha contract. Then I flew to Doha to sign the contract with QGPC.

With the legal details settled, the execution phase began. A plan had already been worked out between the Zakhem company and our Qatari agent, Jassem Jaidah. Together, Zakhem and Jaidah had formed a local Qatari company managed by Zuheir Boulos, who was then a Senior Engineer with Darwih Engineering. Our Qatari registered company was called Med-gulf Construction Est. (Mediterranean-Gulf Construction Est.). I acted as Chairman and Zuheir Boulos, who held a small share, was Managing Director.

Professionally, the first three months of 1976 were full of excitement and hard work. Personally, my primary concern was to relocate my wife and two sons, who were still in Cairo at the time. I was back in Lebanon in mid-February when there was a lull in the fighting thanks to talks held in Damascus that brought together representatives of the various Lebanese factions, in the hope that agreement would be reached to end all hostilities in Lebanon. Many Lebanese were hopeful that this peace process would lead to a permanent settlement. Lisa and I discussed matters at length, and we decided that she should return with our family to Beirut. But the truce was short-lived. In early March, General Aziz El Ahdab led a coup against the President of the Republic of Lebanon. The putsch ended in failure and its only result was ending the fragile ceasefire. Once again, air traffic in and out of Lebanon ceased and it became extremely difficult to communicate with anyone in the country. Lisa and I decided that Beirut was too dangerous. Through contacts in the Lebanese government, I arranged for my wife and children to be taken to the airport by Lebanese security personnel, where they were lucky enough to get on one of the few flights to London.

By April 1976, we were settled in our new London home and had enrolled our boys in a private English school. During this period, I continued to travel monthly to the Middle East and Africa on business. These trips usually lasted two weeks or so, but I could not visit Beirut because of the war. At this time, like most Lebanese who had fled their country, we expected that the war would not last more than a few weeks or months. We remembered how Lebanon had been struck by turmoil in 1958 and how that situation was resolved after about six months. By late 1976, however, Lisa and I realised that Lebanon's war would not end soon, and so we made plans for a five-year stay in London.

The Zakhem business would also have to plan to conduct all its activities from its London offices for the long-term. With this fact in mind, I acquired a building for the company at 2 Queen's Gate Terrace, SW7, and converted part of it into offices. The top two floors became my family's residence. We moved into the new premises in 1978. We liked the area and the environment, which was very different from what we had experienced in North London. Our children were enrolled at Hill House School in Kensington. Lisa was happy with our new home, not least because it was located close to Harrods and the other fashionable stores in Knightsbridge and Sloane Street. Our house was near other landmarks such as Hyde Park, Albert Hall, and Imperial College. We were also part of London's growing Lebanese community, which meant we could socialise with our compatriots.

In April 1976, our company was awarded the Mombasa–Nairobi pipeline project in Kenya. My brother Abdallah moved to Nairobi to execute the contract. Both of us were impressed by Kenya, and we decided to establish our regional office for East Africa in Nairobi. We moved some of our staff from Beirut to our new Kenyan headquarters. Most of the construction equipment we needed was imported, all new, from Japan. We also purchased two Bell helicopters from the United States that we used for aerial inspection of the pipeline.

Crisis, Success and Honour

By September, our projects in Kenya and Qatar were progressing satisfactorily. We sought additional work in Qatar, and secured a project with CE Natco to construct four wellhead treatment plants at Fahaheel on behalf of QGPC. It was a sheer coincidence that the consulting engineer was Pencol Engineering Consultants, also of the UK. Working from my office in London, I was able to monitor progress on both of our projects in Qatar.

Although pleased with my business successes, I nevertheless was constantly worried about conditions at home in Lebanon. People were dying every day by the hundreds. My parents had to leave their home in Deddeh because of the fighting. They sought refuge in Homs, Syria, with my brother Ibrahim. At that time, Ibrahim was overseeing our operations in Syria. Later, I made arrangements for my parents to visit us in London. It was their first experience of air travel and they were happy to stay with us for a few weeks. My father did not want to stay longer because he was anxious to return to his village to check on friends and to look after his properties and business generated by his olive oil press. Also, my father was not a great fan of London, and he was bored with everything because he did not speak English. On the other hand, my mother was happy to be in a peaceful city with her son and his family, especially her grandchildren, and she wanted to stay longer. My father returned to Lebanon, but my mother – after some additional weeks in London – travelled on to Venezuela where she visited my sister, Najibah and her family. Najibah had been living in Caracas since her marriage in 1970 to Richard Isa, an engineer. This trip was special for my mother because she had not yet met Najibah's three daughters.

On January 16th 2008, my sister Najibah passed away at the age of 68 after suffering from a serious illness. She was visiting her daughter Ana-Maria in Toronto, Canada, who is married and blessed with a one year old son. Her two other daughters, Alexandra and Leila, left Caracas, Venezuela, a few years ago and are living and working in Toronto. My sister, Georgette, and her family also live there. Lisa and I attended the funeral in Toronto where Najibah was buried.

* * *

Starting in 1978, we began a family tradition under which the various and far-flung branches of the Zakhem family would converge in Nairobi to spend the Christmas holiday together. My brother Abdallah – who was still a bachelor and had a large house with a big garden, swimming pool, tennis court, and other amenities – served as host. My two sons loved visiting Africa and especially enjoyed flying in the company's helicopters over our construction projects. Also, we visited wildlife lodges like the one at Masai Mara and spent time at the famous Mount Kenya Safari Club Resort.

The Mount Kenya Safari Club Resort was the most luxurious hotel in Africa, comparable to any such facility in the world. The famous Hollywood actor William Holden had opened the resort in the late 1950s on a parcel of land at the foot of Mount Kenya. An animal reserve consisting of thousands of acres was located nearby. A working film studio was located on the grounds of the resort; the film *Mogambo* was made there as well as several other movies about Africa. Given its connections to Hollywood, the resort was a favoured haunt of famous Hollywood actors, producers, and directors, as well as other international jetsetters. In the early 1980s, I met the famous producer David Lean there. In 1977, the Saudi businessman Adnan Khashogji purchased the resort and ran it for ten years until his fortunes collapsed.

I first met Adnan Khashogji during the Christmas season of 1978. Lisa and I were invited to attend a large luncheon at his private ranch. It took about thirty minutes to reach the Khashogji ranch by aeroplane departing from the Mount Kenya Safari Club Resort. At this event, around 100 guests from all over the world drank martinis and champagne before being served an elegant lunch. Adnan was famous for his generosity and hospitality. He made his guests feel at home, practically like members of his extended family. After the lunch, we were assigned four-wheel drive safari cars so we could tour the ranch and observe all kinds of animals such as lions, leopards, and zebras. After that luncheon party, I never met Adnan Khashogji again except on two or three occasions when Lisa and I were invited to private parties hosted by friends in London.

Kenya has historical connections to the Arab world. The coastal region of the country down to Dar es Salaam and the island of Zanzibar in Tanzania was, for a long period of time, under the influence of the Omani Arabs. Trade was conducted between the East African coastal towns and Arabia. The Omanis left their mark on the East African language, Swahili, which has a mixture of Arabic and African words. They also left a striking influence on the architectural design of houses and buildings that is apparent, in particular, in Zanzibar.

Unlike West and South Africa, there were very few Lebanese in East Africa and hardly any in Kenya. We took it upon ourselves to promote good relations between Kenya and Lebanon, and to this end we invited members of the press, politicians, and businessmen from Lebanon to visit the country. On one such visit I invited a group of friends and their families to spend Christmas and the New Year (1978–9) in Kenya. This group included the Deputy Speaker of the Lebanese Parliament, Michel Maalouli, and the owner and Chief Editor of the Arab weekly news magazine *Al Hawades*, Salim El Losi. Salim was also the owner/editor of the English language weekly, *The Events*. *Al Hawades* and *The Events* were published in London at Harrington Gardens, a stone's throw from where I lived. These two reputable magazines were not printed at this time in Beirut because of the war. This was a shame because *Al Hawades* was widely read and often quoted by Arab and international media.

We arranged for Salim El Losi to meet the President of Kenya, Mzee Jomo Kenyatta, his Vice-President Daniel Toroitich arap Moi, and his Foreign Minister Njoroge Mungai. Salim conducted interviews with these men and published them in his magazines. In addition, he published two major articles about our company's operations in Kenya and East Africa. These articles were complimentary of the company in general and also of me personally.

Salim El Losi was a writer and editor of integrity who was highly critical of most Arab regimes. He expressed his views in blunt weekly editorials published in the pages of his magazines. He strongly criticised the failure of the Arab governments to find a solution to the raging war in Lebanon. Salim stated the facts irrespective of the consequences they may have had on his publications or on himself. Almost inevitably, the Beirut headquarters of *Al Hawades* were bombed and burned in 1977. Threats against Salim's life were routine. For this reason he moved his operation to London and resumed publishing in the same courageous spirit. His approach also paid off in business terms: sales of his magazine increased markedly. Although threats against his life continued to be made, Salim refused to alter his style or diminish his criticism. Tragically, in March 1980 – after spending a week in Lebanon to attend his mother's funeral – a gang of armed men kidnapped him as he was on his way to Beirut airport. Three days after he disappeared, Salim's mutilated body was found beside a road on the outskirts of Beirut. He had even been burned with acid. With Salim's death, the Arab world lost a great journalist and an independent, critical voice.

* * *

In 1979, in appreciation of the services our company had rendered on behalf of Lebanese interests in Kenya, Lebanon's government appointed my brother Abdallah as its Honorary Consul in Nairobi. We established a Lebanese consulate adjacent to our offices in Kenya, and it still operates to this day. Abdallah's appointment reflected the excellent relationships we maintained at all times with the Kenyan authorities. Specifically, we helped promote Lebanese investment in important Kenyan sectors such as tourism, agriculture, and trade. More recently, one of our company's former employees was appointed as Honorary Consul of Kenya in Lebanon.

Our work in Africa helped our company to grow and expand. Directly after completing the Mombasa-Nairobi oil pipeline, we secured another major project: the Mombasa and coastal water distribution system. This was a project of great importance for our company as it was the largest in value, $45,000,000, and the first to be awarded to our company by the World Bank. Around the same time, we resumed work at Dar es Salaam, Tanzania, on a small project for the Tazama Oil Company. By the end of 1979, we had tendered for major pipeline projects in both Nigeria and Libya.

As early as 1978 we had decided to open an office in Houston because that city was rapidly gaining a reputation as the energy centre for the United States and the world. All major oil companies had their headquarters, or were represented, in Houston. In turn, manufacturing, engineering, and construction companies for the oil and gas industries were also present in that city. Since we wanted to develop our business in the Middle East and North Africa, it became important to establish ourselves in Houston as well. We therefore registered Zakhem Engineering International Inc. and opened offices at 2 Allen Center in downtown Houston. I appointed

Maurice H. Zakhem, a relative of ours, as the area representative until his early retirement in the mid-1980s. Maurice had left Lebanon due to the civil war to seek a better future for himself and his family. Two of his brothers and their families had already moved to the US, and Maurice decided to go there as well. Today, our operations in Houston are successfully managed under the able leadership of my son Salim.

Our operations in Houston afforded us the opportunity to acquire new knowledge and a better understanding of the oil industry. We not only gained more experience in selecting the latest and most advanced construction equipment for a particular project, but we learned how to do so on better terms. We were also able to establish direct contact with oil companies operating in Africa and the Middle East, as well as with manufacturers of material and equipment.

One of the greatest outcomes of establishing our business ventures in the US was the opportunity it provided for me to meet a number of American Lebanese who have contributed to the progress of the state of Texas. I was humbled, but also very proud, to meet the world famous heart surgeon Dr Michael DeBakey; leading earth scientist Mr Michel T. Halbouty; Tom Younis, a distinguished lawyer with one of the most successful legal practices in Dallas; Fred Rizk, a real estate developer who played an important role in the growth and expansion of various locations in Houston; and Louis Macy, a member of the Council of the City of Houston. I have also come to know about J. M. Haggar, who created a world-wide business in the clothing industry; and Joe Jamail, one of the top lawyers in Houston whose 'claim to fame' was winning the case against Texaco for Penzoil in the late 1980s for four billion dollars.

Forty years after the Zakhem company was established, it is possible to measure our growth in terms of three decades: in the 1960s, we flourished mostly in Iraq; in the 1970s, we grew by working in Qatar and Kenya; and during the early 1980s, we succeeded in gaining a key contract: the Mesla Oilfield Development Project in Libya. The project included the supply and construction of 600 kilometres of pipeline extending from Mesla oilfield to Benghazi and two major pumping stations. To facilitate completion of this work, we acquired for the first time an executive jet, specifically a Learjet 35A, which we used to commute between London, Benghazi, and Beirut.

Our entry into the Libyan market was most opportune, if we take into account the scale of activity in the country's oil sector and the scarcity of contractors operating there. After completing the Mesla project, we decided to establish a major presence in Libya and launched Zakhem International Libya Ltd. In January 1983, immediately after establishing our Libyan branch, we received letters of intent for two pipeline projects. Our Libyan fortunes, however, soon soured because of politics.

The issue first came to our attention in an ominous manner: as my brother Abdallah tried to fly into Benghazi on our company's Learjet, his aeroplane was denied permission to enter Libyan airspace. At the same time, the Libyan authorities ordered us to cease activities, repatriate our entire Lebanese workforce, and terminate our operations in Benghazi within fifteen days. We were not given an explanation for these precipitous actions. After making enquiries, we discovered the source of our troubles. During a summit meeting of 'non-aligned' countries, Libya's leader, Colonel Qaddafi, had a fierce argument with Lebanese President, Amine Gemayel. The day after this confrontation, Libya decided to terminate the work of all Lebanese companies operating on its territory. This was a real blow to our company.

As a result of the Libyan crackdown, we were faced with two immediate problems: the need to temporarily extend the stay of our Lebanese staff to complete work in hand, and to dispose of our camps and equipment with minimal loss. We asked our Libyan client to intervene on our behalf with their government. As a result of this approach, our Lebanese staff in Libya were allowed to remain in the country for two months instead of two weeks. Regarding our camps and equipment in Libya, however, we received no satisfaction. We were forced into one-sided negotiations with a buyer, the National Services of Petroleum Company (NSPC), a subsidiary of National Oil Company, who then basically commandeered the equipment with the help of a policeman. More than two decades later, our company has not yet received payment for the construction equipment that was seized in Libya. A Libyan court ruling declared that the Zakhem company should be paid the money it is owed – around $10,000,000 since 1983 – but to this date the court's ruling has not been carried out.

The Libyan incident was a severe setback for our business. In addition to the income and equipment that were immediately lost, we also had to shelve our long-term plan to grow by means of operating in the Libyan market. As luck would have it, just as we were thrown out of Libya, our operations in Kenya and Qatar were slowing down. In Kenya, we had just completed a major job – the Nairobi City Water Supply and Distribution project – and we had no project of a similar magnitude in sight. Our partner in Qatar, Jassem Jaidah, hinted that he would like to buy our share in Medgulf Construction Est., and I agreed. The deed of sale was finalised at the end of 1982. This was the end of our involvement in construction projects in the Gulf States for many years. We made the strategic decision to concentrate our growth in Lebanon and Africa. Around this time, I also began to invest in property development in Britain and Portugal.

The early 1980s were turbulent years for the Zakhem company, just as they were for Lebanon. In May 1982, the Israeli army invaded Lebanon and by August had reached the outskirts of Beirut. After laying siege to the city and bombarding it from land, sea, and air, the Israelis entered and occupied the city. Having suffered heavy losses in the fighting and facing acute diplomatic pressure, including pressure from the United States, Israel eventually withdrew from Beirut and the surrounding areas but remained in the south of Lebanon. A multinational force tried to help the weakened Lebanese central government to maintain a degree of law and order, but various Lebanese militias grew quite powerful as the Lebanese army experienced a near-total collapse. As part of a larger plan to reassert its authority, the Lebanese government, under President Amine Gemayel, announced an emergency plan to reconstruct Beirut and other areas destroyed by the war. To implement this plan, a new Board for Reconstruction and Development was created, and pledges of financial assistance were obtained from foreign governments.

* * *

Since 1965 when Zakhem Construction completed two projects in the south of Lebanon, it had been my policy not to do any work in Lebanon under contract from the Lebanese government. This policy was altered after the Israeli occupation of Lebanon in 1982, when the Board for Reconstruction and Development was formed.

Dr Kamal A. Shair owner of Dar Al Handasa, a large engineering and consulting firm, proposed that we should get involved in the reconstruction of Lebanon now that Israel was being forced by the Security Council to withdraw. The Zakhem company believed that, as a Lebanese company, it was duty-bound to do all it could to help Lebanon rebuild. Unfortunately, our hopes for a new way of doing business were dashed; only a few months into the new reconstruction contracts, we discovered that official corruption and mismanagement were still the norm. Three months after our company received a contract to build two roads, President Gemayel ordered the Chairman of the Board for Reconstruction and Development, Dr Mohammed Attallah, to take the contract public, thereby contradicting the terms of the original contract signed between us and the Board. As a result of this action and various other reasons, Dr Attallah resigned his position. For our part, we had already mobilised and had started working on site, but were never paid or compensated for what we had done.

Faced with this situation and as we were about to take our case to court, Dr Shair organised a meeting for me with President Amine Gemayel in his presence in August 1983. The President tried to explain to me why his government had, in effect, cancelled our contract. He admitted that an injustice had been done to our company in this matter. Later on, in light of further discussions, we decided not to go to court. Instead, we decided to seek other contracts that could compensate us for some of our losses, and we were able to secure two road construction projects shortly thereafter.

Later on we secured other contracts for road construction in Lebanon. Yet once again, due to official corruption and open hostility between warring Lebanese factions the following year (1984), we were forced to cease work and were officially terminated by the government. Around this time, the Lebanese pound went into steep decline in relation to the US dollar. This currency devaluation was also a major blow to our company. Nevertheless, around this time Zakhem purchased a major Lebanese bank and managed to expand its operations even in the midst of the turmoil and uncertainty that had enveloped the whole country.

In 1992, after the Taef Agreement was concluded, which basically ended the Lebanese civil war, we were again invited by the Lebanese Board of Construction and Development to bid for government contracts. After making enquiries with our official contacts, Zakhem Construction was assured that Prime Minister Rafic Hariri would personally guarantee that the government would fulfil the terms of each and every official contract. Despite these assurances that were made to me personally by Dr Kamal Shair, I was not convinced and so informed my brothers, Albert and Abdallah. They, however, disagreed with my view and maintained greater confidence in the new Lebanese administration. Frankly, by this time I was simply allergic to doing business with the Lebanese government in any way, shape, or form. I did not object, however, to executing private (non-government) contracts, and so we were involved with the construction of a new Lebanese American University (LAU) campus at Byblos starting in 1988.

Arguing in favour of my brothers' view that we should do business with the Lebanese government was the fact that our company had successfully worked in some of the most difficult countries in the world, including Iraq, Libya, and Nigeria, so surely we could do the same for the benefit of our own country. And so I reluctantly agreed that we should seek official contracts from the Lebanese government. The one factor motivating my decision not to get involved was that there are few companies that are deeply rooted and really know how to operate in Lebanon where maintaining close working relations with the government is vital. Most companies doing business with the Lebanese government sign a contract and then immediately assign lawyers to monitor progress. Naturally, company lawyers correspond with the government purely on a legal level. When a dispute arises, work on the site is interrupted and may totally stop until the issue is resolved through negotiation or in court. Even if the contractor eventually resumes work, the project suffers and invariably is not completed either on time or within budget.

In our company we followed a different policy: we focused on doing the work and avoided legal wrangling. For example, throughout our forty-two years in business, Zakhem Construction resorted to international arbitration only once. Normally, we complete a job, hand it over to the party that hired us, and then sit down with the consulting engineer and the client to resolve any outstanding disputes in accordance with FIDIC (Fédération Internationale des Ingénieurs Conseils) standards. This approach, however, did not work well in the case of Lebanon because the government maintains its own standards separate from those of FIDIC.

Unfortunately, the assurances we received from the new Lebanese government did not reflect what actually happened. Of the five projects we executed under contract, only one ended amicably. The other four ended up in court, and we are awaiting the court's judgment to this day. In the process we spent over $40,000,000 to finance the jobs and complete them on time. This was a serious ordeal, but our company survived thanks to its status as an international company: our successes in other countries, in effect, subsidised our losses in Lebanon. One of the worst aspects of doing business in our own country was the fact of facing enormous difficulties – difficulties that we had never faced anywhere else outside Lebanon. Emotionally and sentimentally, I truly wished to contribute substantially to the reconstruction of Lebanon, but the difficulties and problems we faced made it impossible to do so.

Beyond our Libyan and Lebanese woes, we sought growth by concentrating on work in Africa. Fortunately, we made good progress in Kenya and Tanzania. In 1983, for example, we secured a major contract to build an oil storage depot on the coast of Mombasa. Around the same time, we built a five-star luxury hotel, also in Mombasa. We also had road projects in both Kenya and Tanzania; later, we built a major road in Botswana. Our work in Botswana involved some professional and personal pain when we discovered that our Managing Director in that country had betrayed our trust by passing the details of our bids to our competitors. Upon investigation, we also learned that he had embezzled hundreds of thousands of dollars from Zakhem and used the money to launch his own company which he used to obtain contract work from our competitors while he was still on our payroll. More shocking than this professional chicanery was the fact that the man in question was my first cousin Nicola Zakhem. What is more, our company paid for his education in the US to get his degree in Engineering. On a personal level, I was taught a very hard lesson that trust and confidence can be betrayed even by people very close to you.

Our campaign to secure projects in West Africa – especially Nigeria – did not bear fruit until 1990. My first attempt to enter the Nigerian market was in 1969, when I visited the country for the first time by invitation of one of my friends, Yousuf Hammoud.

He operated a flourishing import-export business in the country. My concern at this time was to obtain as much information as I could about Nigeria's oil industry and its prospects for the future. Companies like McDermot, Mothercat, and Wilbros were operating in Nigeria on a large scale. From my travels and conversations, it was clear that Nigeria might be a promising market for the Zakhem company, but we needed to establish ourselves locally and in accordance with Nigerian law, which I discovered later was not an easy thing to do. I made two follow-up visits to the country in 1970, but ultimately I decided that my Nigerian plans would have to be postponed. I never dropped my Nigerian aspirations, though, and closely followed the development of the country. In 1977, we tendered our first contract for a gas pipeline project, but we were not successful. Later, in the 1980s, we made two other submissions on other projects, and again we failed.

It was not until 1990 that we had our first breakthrough in Nigeria. The Nigerian National Petroleum Company (NNPC) announced a major project to lay over 2,000 kilometres of pipeline. Three contracts were to be awarded on an engineering procurement and construction (EPC) basis. The Nigerian authorities asked interested contractors to submit pre-qualification documents by October 1st 1990. We submitted our documents in a joint venture with Kawasaki Steel Corporation of Japan under the name Zakhem Kawasaki JV. Our plan was for Zakhem to do the construction work while Kawasaki handled engineering and procurement. NNPC determined that Zakhem Kawasaki JV was a qualified bidder and we sought contract Number 3, which was the largest. This contract entailed laying 850 kilometres of pipelines and constructing two oil storage depots with storage tanks, pumps, and truck fill-stands. Our tender price was submitted on March 25th 1991, to the amount of $206,000,000. Our price was the lowest among the five bidders and 25 per cent below the next lowest.

After six months of post-tender negotiations on technical and commercial matters, the consulting engineers, Messrs Penspen International of Britain, along with the NNPC project team, submitted their final report to the Board of Directors of NNPC for approval. The Board, however, did not approve the recommendation of the tender committee because they believed that our price was too low. In addition, the NNPC Board thought our company was too small to sustain such a project. At the same time, the Board instructed their project team to negotiate with the second lowest contractor, Entrepose of France, and award them the contract within fifteen days. News of these developments came to me via our agent in Lagos, and, naturally, I took it as a major blow. I interrupted an ongoing business meeting in my office in London so that I could take the time to think things through.

I decided to send a letter of appeal to the Nigerian Minister of Petroleum in his capacity as Chairman of NNPC. My letter would: (1) assert our entitlement to the contract, thus saving a tremendous sum of money for the government and people of Nigeria; and (2) assure the Minister of the financial and technical capabilities of our consortium. I also asked to meet with the Minister so that I could explain our position in person. Before sending my letter, I informed Kawasaki and obtained their approval in writing for my course of action. I also consulted with my friend Ely Calil, who had a wide circle of contacts in Nigeria, and asked for his help. He assured me that the Minister was a person of goodwill who would grant me a fair hearing.

I faxed my letter and, sure enough, was given an appointment with the Minister at his office at the NNPC headquarters. I arrived in Lagos two days ahead of the meeting and made contact with a few people to obtain their advice on certain critical details. Although some of my contacts urged me to be cautious, I was determined to do everything possible to obtain the contract that we had already won in principle. During my meeting with the Minister, he listened to my points carefully and posed pertinent questions that demonstrated that he was well informed about the matter being discussed. In short, he was convinced of our ability to construct the pipeline.

The Minister showed the greatest concern about our financial reserves. He asked, 'What about the financial responsibility? You state that your partners in the consortium, Kawasaki, are capable and from what I see in their financial statement they are very much so. But they haven't countersigned your letter to me. Could you get an authenticated letter from them within the next forty-eight hours certifying that they are jointly responsible with the Zakhem company towards NNPC and that they do support the consortium financially? With this letter in hand I can present your case to the Board during our next meeting.' I responded that I could indeed obtain such a letter and took my leave.

I immediately contacted Kawasaki in Tokyo and asked them to despatch the required letter immediately. The Commercial Attaché with the Japanese embassy in Lagos hand delivered the letter to the Minister before the specified deadline. Now, all I could do was await the internal deliberations of the NNPC. Shortly after the NNPC Board met, I was informed that they had reconsidered the bid tendered by the Zakhem-Kawasaki consortium. We had indeed obtained the contract! I was elated, called a celebratory dinner with some close colleagues, and left for London to begin work on this important project.

We received a letter of intent on September 15th and replied to NNPC, albeit with certain reservations, on the 23rd. The Zakhem-Kawasaki team was now in Lagos negotiating a draft of the contract with NNPC. Towards the end of November, it was agreed that the contract signature would take place on a certain date in December. The leader of the Kawasaki team advised us that his Managing Director would arrive from Tokyo for this important event. Two days before our team was scheduled to leave London for Lagos to sign the contract, the Kawasaki team leader unexpectedly walked into my office to say that he had received instructions to leave for Tokyo without finalising negotiations and signing the contract with NNPC. 'Who is replacing you and what about the contract signature?' I asked. He remained deadly silent for a moment and then responded, 'These are my instructions and I have to obey them.' He then said, 'I'm sure you will receive something in writing on this subject from the new General Manager of the company.' My interlocutor excused himself, saying, 'I want to thank you, Mr Zakhem, as I have to leave now to go with my three engineers to the airport to board our flight to Tokyo.' I asked: 'Will I see you again or hear from you?' 'No,' he said, 'I'm being moved to another company within our group which is involved in domestic water works.' I could hardly stand up to shake hands with the fellow.

This was the second bombshell that had exploded on our Nigerian venture. Thinking the worst, it appeared to me that our partners were shying away from the Nigerian contract. The paramount question I faced was what could be done to retrieve the situation. Shortly thereafter, we received a letter from Kawasaki GM Tokyo informing us about their staff changes and requesting us to arrange a meeting with NNPC to re-negotiate the terms of the contract. Kawasaki went on to say that the signature of the contract would depend on the outcome of the next round of negotiations. I could detect from this letter that Kawasaki were endeavouring to avoid signing a contract, but I did not know why.

It was simply impossible for me to tell NNPC that Kawasaki now wanted to negotiate further. Our only alternative solution was to convince the new management of Kawasaki to sign the original contract. We decided that my brother Abdallah should visit Tokyo to discuss the matter face-to-face with them. In the meantime, I would return to Lagos to finalise all other matters so that the contract could be signed.

After holding discussions in Tokyo with Kawasaki, Abdallah could obtain no satisfaction and reported to me on the failure of his mission. My worst fears were confirmed: Kawasaki was trying to extricate itself from a contract it no longer wanted. It looked like the Nigerian contract was lost once and for all. Then I came to the conclusion that we did not need Kawasaki to obtain the NNPC contract. The key step was getting NNPC to open a line of credit equivalent to the total amount of the contract, thus allowing us to work alone. After many negotiating sessions, NNPC agreed to sign a contract with the Zakhem company alone and did indeed grant us the required line of credit. The decision of the Minister of Petroleum, in his capacity as Chairman of NNPC, to grant us the contract was not only courageous but it was also wise as this course of action ultimately saved the country $50,000,000.

Now that we had the contract at last, it was time to take the steps necessary to execute it, including the provision of a performance bond, an advance payment guarantee, insurance, mobilisation, and material procurement. We approached several banks in London, but none of them showed an interest in our work in Nigeria. Finally, American Express Bank indicated a degree of interest and we went through long and tedious scrutiny to satisfy their concerns. We had successfully obtained a credit line of approximately $43,000,000. Ultimately, the Nigerian project was completed in 1995, on time, and we gained an excellent reputation with our client.

In sum, I would say our Nigerian project was a great test of our determination, commitment, and resilience. It was an uphill struggle, and certainly a great challenge to me personally. We had to cross several hurdles and tackle major difficulties on a long and tedious path. I acted in accordance with my first intuition and at every point I found the right people to provide assistance. I am a great believer in dreams. It has been said that 'people who can dream, can do', and I did both.

In 1988, I was elected President of the Board of Directors of the International Pipeline Contractors Association (IPLCA). During my presidency we made plans to amend the organisation's by-laws so as to allow offshore contractors to become members. As part of this process, we were engaged in drafting a new Standard Form of Contract that would be available for all members to use as a model when negotiating contracts with their clients. I was also engaged in planning IPLCA's next convention, which I wanted to hold in Singapore.

Organising the IPLCA's Singapore convention was a truly monumental task. This was to be the organisation's first convention held in the Far East. As President of the Board, I felt that we should convene at a location outside of Europe to demonstrate that we were truly an international association. In addition to a symbolic locale, the selection of speakers was also of great importance. Out of four addresses, I arranged for two to be delivered by prominent Lebanese-Americans. One was Michel Halbouty who was highly respected by all the major oil companies for his knowledge and foresight. The other Lebanese-American speaker was Clovis Maksoud, the permanent representative of the Arab League at the UN and in Washington, DC. Both of these gentlemen were close friends of mine and they agreed to go to Singapore. The other two speakers were experts in the fields of offshore and onshore pipeline construction.

One of my main concerns regarding the Singapore convention of IPLCA was making the necessary arrangements for the President's Reception and Dinner, which was to be held at the National Museum. Over 100 guests were present at this event, most of them company Directors and former Presidents. Other dignitaries, like the Mayor of Singapore were also in attendance. A myriad of details had to be decided, down to the food and drink to be served, and my wife, Lisa, aided me immeasurably.

The President's Reception and Dinner were followed the next

day by an open meeting for all members and guests. I called this meeting to order with a short speech about the future of our industry and welcomed everyone, especially our guest speakers.

The next day an open meeting was scheduled in the morning, and featured a panel discussion on various problems facing our membership in executing their contracts. That evening, there was a black tie dinner during which the sitting board handed leadership over to the newly elected board.

Throughout the week-long Singapore convention, my head was spinning amid a great deal of frantic activity. I would leave my hotel room at 7:00 a.m., return briefly to change clothes, but never retire until after midnight. The activities and meetings I attended included official breakfasts, lunches, and dinners. On numerous occasions I had to address the guests with a few words of welcome and thanks for attending. My presidential address took place during the first session, when most of the attendees were present. Other speakers addressed themes related to our industry. One exception was Dr Clovis Maksoud, who spoke about the state of the Middle East and regional politics in the aftermath of the Iran-Iraq war, which had just come to an end.

The Singapore convention was the culmination of my year-long term as the President of IPLCA, which was amended to become IPLOCA (International Pipeline and Offshore Contractors Association) after allowing offshore companies to become members. During the convention's closing banquet, I introduced the incoming Board and officers. My successor as President of the Board was Walter Zimmermann of Preussag, Germany. Walter came to the podium with his wife, Crystal, and I congratulated him on his election. To this day, I enjoy being a former President of the Association and Lisa and I attend its conventions whenever we can.

Based on opinions expressed by the membership, the 1989 Singapore convention was one of the most successful conventions in the history of the IPLOCA. Recently, I have heard that there is an interest in holding another convention there, and if that happens I will certainly attend as it would bring back many fond memories.

CHAPTER 9

Diversification and Investments

By the 1980s, the Zakhem company had generated more than respectable reserves of cash. This meant that we could afford to invest in capital-intensive projects, provided of course they would benefit our group as a whole. Property development was an attractive option, and I began to invest in this sector in London. Eventually, we also sought opportunities in the US, Kenya, and Portugal.

We were very successful in London because we selected specific projects at prime locations. The first was the old YMCA hostel at Endell Street, WC2. We acquired it in 1979, refurbished the facility, and reopened it as a modern hostel with 100 bedrooms and a cafeteria. Next, we acquired three major properties at Old Brompton Road, SW7; Chitty Street, W1; and Lambourne Avenue, Wimbledon. We constructed a mix of residential buildings on the first and second sites and we built six quality homes on the Wimbledon site. Property development was proving to be a wise investment because it created growth and profits for the company.

One of our investments, the Millennium Windsor-Slough hotel project, was a great achievement for me personally. Having tracked trends in the London property market, I asked Constantinos Nicola – Managing Director of Zakhem Construction UK Ltd – to conduct a survey of all properties that were for sale along both sides of the M25 motorway, specifically the sector between the M4 and M23 motorways. My intuition was that as soon as the M25 motorway opened, the properties in that area would increase in value. As luck would have it, my judgment and foresight were correct but not my timing: we discovered that various real estate companies already held the properties that had caught my attention. There was, however, one parcel of land owned by Slough Council on the M4 at exit Windsor-Slough that looked promising. The Council was willing to sell the property if the buyer committed to building a hotel on it.

I was very interested in this opportunity and instructed Constantinos Nicola to negotiate its purchase. We finalised a deal with the Council. Sometime later, we formed a partnership with Copthorne Hotels under whose name we built a 219-room hotel; the agreement stipulated that Zakhem Construction UK Ltd would be responsible for all matters pertaining to construction, while Copthorne Hotels would handle the finances and operation management on completion. In 1989, the hotel had an enormously successful opening, and I received congratulations from His Royal Highness the Duke of Edinburgh during the inauguration ceremony. Knowing I was from Lebanon, the Duke of Edinburgh said to me, 'You had to come all the way from the Lebanon to show them how to complete a project on time!' From the day of its opening, the hotel became one of the two top performing hotels operated by the Copthorne group. We sold our interest in the company ten years later at a handsome profit. The project was a major success in more than one way. It gave a deeper meaning to the work we were doing; it gave us something that went beyond material success. This experience, in fact, filled us with a new spirit and a sense of profound confidence that we do possess the tenacity, the determination, and the ingenuity to explore new areas and undertake new projects.

Every property development project we have undertaken has been carefully studied and meticulously executed. A recent effort was the development of 24 Kensington Gore, located adjacent to Hyde Park in London. We negotiated for about three years with the Council of the Borough of Westminster to obtain their approval for a building permit. From the outside, the property looks like a nineteenth-century building with constituted stone and red brick facades that match the character of the surrounding buildings. The cost of building per square foot was approximately £300. This building, thanks to its special features, stands as a landmark at Kensington Gore near the Royal Albert Hall, overlooking Kensington Gardens and the Prince Albert Monument. I decided to keep the penthouse as my residence.

In keeping with our planning, I had an opportunity to invest in a tourist and leisure project in the Algarve, Portugal. Schroder Asseily Ltd, a financial house in London, proposed that we participate in a joint venture with one of their major clients, Beach Villas Ltd, to develop around 400 acres of land in the Algarve. The project comprised building a holiday town with an eighteen-hole

29 The day in 1964 when I decided to start our own company; with my brother Abdallah
30 Forty-four years afterwards, with Abdallah in 2009
31 Viewing the construction of an oil-storage-terminal project at Tema, Ghana
32 The topping-out ceremony, with the Mayor of Slough, for the Windsor Slough Millennium Hotel

33 As the president of the Board of Directors, with all the members of the IPLOCA Board in 1988 **34** With my friend, Michel Halbouty, and his wife Billye **35** With Clovis Maksoud (*left*) and Michel Halbouty (*right*), two distinguished speakers at the 1989 IPLOCA convention **36** With my wife and the welcoming committee at the IPLOCA convention in Singapore – 1989 **37** Delivering the keynote address at the 1989 IPLOCA convention

38 (*left to right*) Dr Riyad Nassar, myself, Dr Michael DeBakey, Dr Philip Salem and Dr Nadim Zacca in 1995

39 On the Cedars of Lebanon mountain; (*left to right*) Mrs DeBakey, myself, Mrs Philip Salem, Dr DeBakey and Olga, his daughter

40 Meeting Dr DeBakey in his office with Dr Philip Salem

41 With Patriarch Ignatius IV (*right*) and Bishop Saliby (*left*) after receiving the Golden Cross of St Peter and St Paul in London – 1955

42 At the President's Palace, Lebanon (2000); (*left to right*) Dr Riyad Nassar, Antoine Frem, myself, President Emile Lahoud, Dr Michael DeBakey, Jurgen Seibke and Dr Nabil Haidar

43 Receiving my honorary doctorate degree from LAU President Nassar (*left*) and Vice-president Haidar in 1995

44 With President Daniel Arap Moi of Kenya **45** With President Abdoulaye Wade of Senegal in 2005
46 With President John Agyekum Kufuor of Ghana **47** With the Nigerian Minister for Oil, Professor J. Amino
48 Signing the first contract with the managing directors of BOST Ghana in 2004, with my son Marwan on the left

49 With Pope John Paul II at the Vatican in 2001
50 With the then Archbishop of Canterbury in London – 2002
51 With HRH the Prince of Wales in London in 2006
52 With HRH the Duke of Edinburgh and my wife in 1991

53 Zakhem Engineering Building, Byblos Campus
54 With my brothers, Abdallah and Albert, in front of the building on dedication day
55 Lebanese American University campus at Byblos

56, 57, 58 The Hannah and Salim Zakhem Building at Balamand University. On the steps, President Elie Salem and myself.

golf course, 200 villas and flats, and a 200-bed hotel. We seized this opportunity and went into the venture on a fifty/fifty basis with the understanding that we would handle construction while our partners did the managing and marketing. Two years later, we inaugurated the golf course and golf club, which is named Forest Park (or Parque da Floresta). It is now one of the most famous resorts in the Algarve. In 1988, we sold our interest in the project and initiated other commercial and residential projects in Lisbon. Along with Schroder Asseily Ltd, we created two major investment funds to support our property development projects. To date, our investments in Portugal have been profitable, but not as lucrative as our London dealings. I believe that the main reason for this state of affairs is that we had few partners and could not take critical decisions rapidly enough.

To the extent permitted by political and security conditions, we never entirely ceased doing business in Lebanon. After the 1982 Israeli invasion of Lebanon, the UN Security Council passed a resolution demanding an immediate Israeli withdrawal and the deployment of a multinational force in Beirut. This international force was charged with the responsibility of helping the Lebanese government maintain law and order. Most of the people of Lebanon at this time were hoping that their country was moving towards peace. It was during this short respite that the Zakhem company decided to invest actively in Lebanon. To do so, we acquired a major share of the Majdaleni Bank, a local concern that was experiencing major liquidity problems.

After four months of negotiations with the Central Bank of Lebanon, we concluded the Majdaleni Bank deal and immediately restructured its operations. First, we changed the name of the bank to Allied Business Bank. A new Board of Directors was constituted that included my brother Abdallah and myself. In keeping with our intention to have banking professionals manage the institution, we selected an old friend, Elias Saba, as Chairman of the Board. Elias is a career economist and had served as Lebanon's Minister of Finance from 1970–72. Abdallah succeeded Elias in 1986 as Chairman, and was elected as President of the Banking Association of Lebanon in 1987 for a period of two years.

A second project in which we were interested around this time was building the Zakhem company headquarters in Beirut. We selected a property in a prestigious location at Sin El-Fil in the eastern sector of the city. There we constructed a 55,000 square-foot building with a 125-space covered car park and 25,000 square feet of gardens. A third project involved purchasing 70 per cent ownership in an existing hotel on the sea front of Beirut, the Riviera Hotel. The hotel, which dates back to 1952, is well known by local Lebanese and tourists visiting Lebanon. Finally, we acquired other properties in various locations in the hope that we would be able to develop them, but alas none of these projects could be completed. Unfortunately, the political situation in Lebanon did not calm down and the country experienced another destructive cycle of violence that lasted until 1990. The United States helped broker an agreement on May 17th 1983, between Lebanon and Israel that called for the withdrawal of Israeli troops and a cessation of the formal state of war between the two countries. This agreement, although signed by representatives of both governments, was not ratified and was never implemented. In February 1983, even as Lebanon continued to experience violence perpetrated by local and international forces, a suicide bomber driving a truck full of explosives attacked the US marines stationed near Beirut airport. Approximately 300 marines were killed. As a result, all US units pulled out of Lebanon along with other multi-national forces. In short, Lebanon was now once again wracked by total and unchecked anarchy.

Three months later, Syrian forces entered Beirut to enforce law and order. The Lebanese leadership and people were bitterly divided between those who favoured the Syrians and those who were against their presence. The airport in Beirut was closed, the economy went into free-fall, and the Lebanese currency lost over 90 per cent of its value. Naturally, our company's interests were affected by these developments, especially our investments in real estate and in the bank. The Central Bank insisted that we make up for capital loss, and I was forced to bring money in from outside sources.

Our headquarters building was put on hold after the concrete structure was completed, while the Riviera Hotel remained in its dilapidated state partly occupied by one of the local militias, thus incurring an operating loss. Closing down the hotel completely would have resulted in having the militia occupy the hotel and take it over by force. To reduce our losses, we decided to operate the hotel as best we could in these very difficult times. The upshot of all this was that my dream of investing in Lebanon collapsed. Personally, I learned that one should not invest money based on emotion, as we had done. Grimly, all I could do was hope that in the future things would improve in my country.

Even as our Lebanese plans fell apart, our operations in other areas continued to develop. The Intercontinental Hotels group approached us to invest in a new 200-room, 5-star hotel they planned to construct on the coast of Mombasa, Kenya. After studying the feasibility of the project and negotiating terms, we signed an agreement in 1982. The Zakhem company provided 40 per cent of the equity for the new company, called Equatorial Beach Property Ltd (EBPL), which was to own the hotel and manage the construction. Intercontinental Hotels underwrote the remaining 60 per cent of the equity and was to manage the operation of the hotel after its completion. Duncan Ndegua, an ex-Governor of the Kenya Central Bank, owned the property. He agreed to exchange the value of the property against equity in the newly formed company, EBPL. Equity was paid and supplemented by two loans from the Industrial Development Bank and the International Finance Corporation.

Construction on the Mombasa hotel began in 1982 and was completed three years later. The hotel opened for business during the Christmas 1985 season, and was formally inaugurated by the President of Kenya in early 1986. The hotel was successful for about two years, but then the AIDS scare greatly harmed the tourism industry in Kenya. Later, in the 1990s, the threat of terrorism in Kenya further hurt local tourism. During this time, many Kenyan hotels filed for bankruptcy. We also had to close our hotel for business in 2001, but with the intention of making a fresh start when the local business climate improved. As of yet, signs of improvement have not yet appeared, so the hotel remains closed.

In the United States the Zakhem company invested in real estate in cities such as New York, Dallas, and Houston. We participated in the development of various projects namely one hotel in New York, two office buildings, and several homes and apartments in Arlington, Texas. Like many others, in the late 1970s we invested in the Texas oil industry. Our oil ventures did not succeed as we hoped, and we have since concentrated on what we know best, namely property development.

CHAPTER 10

My Family

As I have described elsewhere, the security situation in Lebanon deteriorated during the 1970s and 1980s as a result of large-scale fighting between various Lebanese factions and their non-Lebanese supporters, including the Palestine Liberation Organization (PLO), the Syrians, and the Israelis. Like many Lebanese, I decided that the safety of my family could only be secured by moving them out of the country. In our case, we were fortunate enough to set up our new home and business offices in London.

Lisa, Salim, and Marwan arrived in London in October 1976 on a Middle East Airlines flight from Beirut. I was anxiously waiting for them at Heathrow Airport. On the way to our flat at Darwin Court, Gloucester Avenue, NW1, I was trying to amuse the boys by telling them about London, but they would interrupt me saying: 'Dad, did you know that the building across from our house in Beirut was hit by a rocket and caught fire? From our balcony we could see members of a certain militia with long beards walking in the street armed with hand grenades and machine guns. At night, we could hear gunfire and explosions!' Lisa quickly intervened by saying, 'Boys, will you please forget all this now as we are here safe and sound and we must look forward to the future.'

We enrolled Salim and Marwan at a private English school near our flat. Our driver would take them in the morning and bring them back around 4:00 p.m. After two years, we took up residence at 2 Queen's Gate Terrace, SW7 and the boys moved to the famous Hill House School at Kensington. After Hill House, we enrolled them both in a boarding school, St Edmund's at Hindhead, Surrey, and after three years they did well in their GCE exams.

In 1982, we were visited by Mrs Leila Saad, the owner and principal of Shuwayfat School in Beirut, together with her deputy Mr Ralph Bustani. They expressed their intention of opening Shuwayfat International School in the UK. They had already acquired a mansion house surrounded by a 100 acres of green virgin land with high trees at Chippenham near the city of Bath. They renovated this house and added a new building which would serve as a dormitory for students. They were also planning to teach courses in the Arabic language during the academic year, and were willing to give private lessons to special students in the summer. We were invited to pay a visit and see the premises for ourselves.

We were highly impressed by what we heard, and became good friends with Leila and Ralph. We were happy to see that a Lebanese school had established itself in the UK and, without any hesitation, Lisa and I decided to move Salim and Marwan to that school to study for their International Baccalaureate, the equivalent of 'A levels'.

At the beginning of the academic year, we drove in our Rolls Royce to the school where we were met by Mrs Saad and Mr Bustani who took us on a tour of the new premises, which included the new dormitory. Each room in the dormitory accommodated two students. The rooms were moderately furnished with two beds, two desks, and two closets. When we asked the boys if they liked the school, they said: 'This is a five-star hotel compared to what we had at St Edmund's.' As we walked around, we met other parents who were visiting the school with their children. We noticed that nearly every car in the parking lot was either a Rolls Royce or a Mercedes which belonged to the visiting parents of the students, most of whom were from the Arab world. Our own car was one of those cars which had a driver waiting to take us back to London.

While at St Edmund's, the boys were allowed to visit home on some weekends, so we used to send the driver to pick them up. The boys were annoyed to see the driver, Montero, coming in the Rolls Royce. As soon as they arrived home, they would ask: 'Why did you send Montero in the Rolls and not in the Volkswagen? Didn't we ask you not to send the Rolls to the school? We feel embarrassed.' At Shuwayfat, however, it was a different story as most cars picking up students were luxurious.

Once we had established ourselves in London and enrolled our children in a local school, my wife Lisa felt somewhat isolated. She was not happy to spend all her time socialising at tea and coffee parties; she wanted to do something useful. In 1978, she formed a partnership with one of our friends to establish a boutique for women called 'Cactus', located in central London. Two years later, she sold her share to her partner, but did not give up the idea of running a business of her own.

Eventually, she asked me to support a business venture she wanted to launch on her own: a jewellery shop located on one of London's fashionable streets. At first I tried to convince her to concentrate on charitable work. Lisa pointed out that she was heavily involved in the British Lebanese Association, and that she wanted to do something else as well. Finally, I agreed and she opened LalaOunis Greek Gold Shop, on Old Bond Street, in September 1985.

At the opening of the shop, senior representatives from famous international jewellers, including Cartier, attended and offered congratulations to Lisa. Ilias LalaOunis was present and made remarks about Greek gold and his approach to design as described in his book *Metamorphoses*. According to LalaOunis, the goldsmith, guided by his imagination, uses his craft to transform ordinary pieces into 'objets d'art'.

For two years, Lisa's business performed well, but it slowed down considerably in the wake of the stock market crash of October 1987. This event was followed by a property market recession in 1989, which had a direct, negative influence on the jewellery trade. By 1990, the business started losing money and I advised Lisa to close shop. She resisted and proposed instead to sell only precious stones. A new agreement was made with the famous jeweller Reposi to market his products. Reposi is well known among the rich and famous for his expensive jewellery formed from precious stones of all kinds. But because of the continuing recession, even this new venture did not succeed. After four years, Lisa decided to close the business and concentrate on her charity work.

A few months before closing her business, Lisa had a horrifying experience. Returning home at 6:00 in the evening from her shop, she walked into the house and went to her bedroom to rest. Three men approached the main door and rang the doorbell. One of them told the maid that he was a flower delivery boy. As the maid opened the door, one of the men, all of whom were wearing masks, hit her with the flowers and ran straight to the main bedroom on the upper floor. Lisa, who had just arrived, was trying to relax sitting on the bed. One of the assailants put a knife to Lisa's throat and demanded to be shown the safe. Lisa pleaded with her attackers not to hurt her and showed them the safe. They opened it, emptied its contents into a pillowcase, and swiftly ran out. The maid called the police, who arrived immediately. I came home fifteen minutes later to find the police with Lisa, who of course was shaken by what had happened. After the incident, Lisa said she could not remain in our residence any longer and so we moved immediately to Thorney Court into a secure building. Later, we moved into our current residence, which I have already described.

With no business to run, Lisa again became more involved in the activities of the British Lebanese Association (BLA). Eventually, she assumed the post of Executive Secretary after the retirement of Leila Tannous Dawton. The main goal of the BLA is fostering understanding and cooperation between the Lebanese and British communities, which it does through a variety of initiatives, including awarding post-graduate scholarships to students from Lebanon to come and study in the United Kingdom. There is no doubt that Lisa's hard work as Chairman of the BLA Fundraising Committee helped to continue its tradition of successful charity work. In 2002, she was named Chairman of the newly formed Lebanese chapter of the English Speaking Union for Lebanon, which she founded with Youmna Asseily.

Given that conditions in Lebanon had settled down, in the mid-1990s we decided to purchase a flat in Beirut on Sorsok Street, Ashrafiyeh. Lisa took responsibility for decorating and furnishing this residence with the assistance of the well-known decorator, Elie Gharzouzy. Our sons Salim and Marwan were working in Beirut and moved into the flat in 1997, while Lisa and I commuted regularly between London and Beirut. Having secured a few contracts in postwar Lebanon, the Zakhem Company re-established offices in our new building at Sin El-Fil.

* * *

After finishing at Shuwayfat, Salim went to Houston, Texas where he attended Texas A&M University at College Station to study engineering. Three years later, he decided to switch majors and study business administration. He then enrolled in St Thomas University where he graduated with a Bachelor's degree. He worked with American Express in London for one year before returning to

St Thomas for his Master's degree. Two years later, he graduated with an MBA and joined a local bank in Hong Kong for a one-year contract. Then he returned to Beirut and joined Allied Business Bank, our bank, but he did not find his work rewarding, and in 1998 he asked me to let him take over our business interests in Houston. I agreed, and, once in Houston, Salim launched an Internet Service Provider company, Tripnet, with the intention to expand in Texas and throughout the US. After one year, the market collapsed, but we persevered until 2003 when the company finally began to generate profit. By the end of 2004, Tripnet improved its ranking to number four in the state of Texas with an impressive performance in revenue and profit.

Salim also acquired a small construction firm that specialised in performing small contracts for the city of Houston. In less than one year, the construction company took jobs valued at around $10,000,000. Given the growth of the firm, Salim asked his brother Marwan to join him. Under Marwan's guidance, in the following year, the company doubled its contracts with the city.

Marwan tried one semester at Texas A&M but he did not like it. He returned to London and enrolled at Imperial College to study engineering. After graduating as a civil engineer in 1994, he joined an American company, Herbert Construction, to work on a project in Cairo for one year. After completing his work there, he moved to Beirut to work with our company and he is now highly ranked in the management of the Zakhem Group.

In 2001, our company was selected to build a new university in Senegal. I had Marwan negotiate the contract, and he did so successfully. He then moved to Senegal and we wrapped up our construction work in Houston. By this time, both Salim and Marwan had left Beirut and were living on two different continents, far away from us. Both our sons were doing well in business and had gained experience working in various countries. Salim had worked in Britain, the US, Hong Kong, and Lebanon; Marwan had experience in Egypt, Lebanon, the US, and Senegal. It is especially gratifying that both my sons had an opportunity to do business in Lebanon. This experience allowed them to relate to their country of origin and associate with their fellow Lebanese.

While living in Dakar, Marwan met a bright and beautiful girl, Lina Khayyat, the daughter of Amer and Mona Khayyat who are

My Family

good friends of ours. Lina also graduated from Imperial College with a degree in Engineering. In 2002, after six months of dating, Marwan proposed and she accepted. That same evening, he announced the news to Lisa and me, and asked for our blessing. We were happy with the news and we expressed our full support.

Marwan and Lina were married at St George's Cathedral in Beirut on the December 28th 2003, and took residence in Dakar after their honeymoon. Six months later, due to the nature of the work that Marwan was pursuing, which involved extensive travel, they moved to London. Unfortunately, shortly thereafter their marriage developed some problems which they could not reconcile. Despite attempts by Lisa and me, and Mr and Mrs Khayyat, to resolve their differences, Marwan and Lina ultimately agreed to an amicable separation in January 2006 and subsequently divorced in October of that year.

Marwan is now fully engrossed with our business in Ghana and Senegal. He is always on the lookout to find new projects in other countries, and is now poised to take on two sizeable projects in Freetown and Monrovia.

Our elder son, Salim, did not feel that he was ready to get married. Instead, Salim was totally engrossed with his ISP company. This venture consumed all his time, with little or nothing left for personal matters. At Marwan's wedding party, however, Salim met his dream girl, Fay Badro, who was seated next to him at the same table all that evening. Her parents were well known to us. He dated her for few months and they seemed to get on very well together. A beautiful and charming girl, Fay graduated from the Lebanese American University in Beirut and then worked in her father's business in Dubai, where she gained valuable experience in the field of international marketing. Her father moved to Dubai from Beirut in the 1970s and started his own company, Greenline, for the furnishing and interior decoration of palaces, homes, and hotels. His business grew steadily and when Fay graduated she joined the company to look after the new business of decorating yachts and large boats. A year after their meeting, Salim and Fay fell in love and decided to get married. They were officially engaged on March 7th 2005 and their wedding was scheduled for early September. We were all very happy and began preparations for the wedding, which was fixed for September 3rd 2005, at the Salle des Étoiles in Monte Carlo.

Although exciting and enjoyable, preparations for the wedding required hard work. My wife Lisa and Fay's mother Nabila worked tirelessly but the onus remained totally on Fay. She worked very hard and made three visits to Monte Carlo: twice with her parents, Lisa, and me, and once on her own. Each time she would spend a week with the management of the Salle des Étoiles to sort out the decorations, arrangements of tables and chairs, the lighting, and other details. The church – the Russian St Nicola Cathedral in Nice – had already been selected by our Metropolite Gabriel Saliby.

Salim and Fay's civil marriage took place on August 17th at Marylebone Town Hall, followed by a lunch at the Ritz Hotel for some fifty relatives and close friends. During the civil ceremony verses from Kahlil Gibran were read by our friend Professor Suheil Bushrui.

The church wedding in Nice took place at 4:00 p.m. and the reception, which was followed by the gala dinner, at the Salle des Étoiles went extremely well. Around 550 guests from all over the world were present. Dr Michael DeBakey, at the age of ninety-seven, together with his wife Katrine flew in especially from Houston to attend. All of the guests complimented us very highly that evening on all aspects of the wedding. They said it matched any Hollywood festivity production and the management of the Salle des Étoiles commented that it was the best wedding they had seen in a long time. Salim and Fay moved to their home in Houston after their honeymoon and are happily living there. On January 14th 2008 they were blessed with the birth of their baby girl, Chloe.

CHAPTER 11

Social and Philanthropic Work

Although I left Lebanon with my family on account of the war, my links with my country were never severed and I used to monitor the news from my homeland every day. Like all Lebanese who settled in London, I was anxious to extend help as far as possible to those who remained behind. During that long war, I received numerous letters from parents seeking financial assistance to enable them to send their children to schools and colleges abroad. Tuition fees in Europe and the US were six times higher than in Beirut, so very few parents could afford to send their children abroad. By their very nature, the Lebanese regard education as the highest priority in life and will make great sacrifices to give their children a good education. As I read letters from parents desperate to educate their children, I remembered the hardships that my own parents endured to put me and my brothers and sisters through school. I also recalled the assistance I received from various sources during my studies at AUB. To help my fellow Lebanese, I instituted, through our company, a student aid fund to benefit a number of deserving students.

* * *

Late in 1982, the President of Beirut University College (BUC), Dr Riyad Nassar, visited me at my office in London. Accompanying him was BUC's Director of Development, Dr Mohamad Yakan. They were seeking a sizeable financial contribution to their institution. After a lengthy meeting, I agreed to establish an endowment fund in the name of my mother to provide scholarships to deserving and needy students. I also agreed to provide additional funding for one or two other students through the Zakhem Student Fund. Early in 1983, President Riyad Nassar extended an invitation to me to join BUC's Board of Trustees, which I accepted. Board meetings were held twice a year in New York and Beirut on a rotating basis. During the war, the Beirut meeting was held in Larnaca or another

European city. The New York meeting was required because BUC is chartered under New York State law and recognised by the New York Board of Regents. I attended my first meeting in the summer of 1983 in Larnaca, Cyprus. During that gathering, I realised just how serious BUC's problems were.

When I joined the BUC Board of Trustees, most of the other members were drawn from the Synod of the Presbyterian Church or were professionals from academia, law, and government. I believe I was the first engineer or businessman to serve on the Board, and so I had a different approach to dealing with the College's crisis. In early 1984, I met with President Nassar to discuss BUC's status. As our meeting came to an end, he asked me if I would succeed Dr Amal Kurban as Chairman of the Board of Trustees. I replied that BUC faced serious problems which would demand great attention on my part and before I could take a decision, I had to make my working plan, and consult with my wife who had graduated from BUC. Three months later, I accepted the invitation to serve as Chairman of the Board. Some of the issues I had to contend with included the following:

- Four of BUC's American professors were taken hostage by Hezbollah ('The Party of God'), a leading Shiite Muslim faction in Lebanon. Continuous negotiations were taking place between the Lebanese government and Hezbollah, but no progress had been achieved by the time I became Chairman of BUC's Board. The professors were eventually released some five years later.

- The BUC campus in Ras Beirut was almost entirely under the control of armed militias. The students expressed their opposition to this dangerous and absurd situation by staging demonstrations and walkouts. The lack of security on campus was illustrated in 1983 when armed members of a militia broke into the house of President Riyad Nassar of BUC. He and his family were eventually released after threats were made by their assailants for demands to be met. As a result of all this intimidation, President Nassar and his family were forced to leave Beirut and seek refuge at their home village of Almunsef, some 95 kilometres from campus. For the next seven years, the President of BUC could not regularly commute to the college campus.

- BUC classes were disrupted on an almost weekly basis by strikes and other political actions called by one political party or another. Similarly, the general lack of security in Lebanon meant that students and faculty could not commute to campus on a regular basis. Absent students, or faculty, or both, meant that it was impossible to maintain a regular academic schedule. Faculty members were forced to give courses extended over the calendar year and at short notice.

- Financially, BUC was in deficit to the amount of $300,000 (over a total budget of $3,000,000). The student body was approximately 2,300 strong, with around 1,000 students on scholarships generously provided by the Hariri Foundation. Other students received scholarships from alternate sources. Because of the war, the US-based foundations and corporations that normally contributed to BUC failed to do so in the belief that, under prevailing conditions, the institution could not possibly operate at even a minimal standard.

- The BUC faculty and staff were demoralised. Over and above the hazards of living and working in a war zone, they were poorly paid even by the prevailing standards in Lebanon at the time. Faculty and staff discontent was not hidden from students, and they in turn became demoralised as well. For their part, management was incapable of effecting positive changes.

The state of BUC as outlined above raised profound and serious questions that required the urgent attention of the Board of Trustees and the President. Surveying the situation of the College, I knew navigating the path ahead would be a tremendous challenge, but I was determined to succeed. To master this situation, I felt, would serve not only the BUC community but also Lebanon as a whole. It has always been my firm belief that education is the best contribution that one can make to the advancement of a people.

In between the BUC Board meetings, I held regular conversations with the BUC leadership, namely President Riyad Nassar, Dean Nabil Haidar, and Director of Development Dr Mohamad Yakan. Our first priority was to solve the institution's financial woes because unless this was done the College would cease to exist. I argued that although lack of security could *disrupt* BUC operations, a financial meltdown would lead to the *disappearance* of the College.

After reviewing the College's finances in detail, I determined that tuition fees paid for approximately 35 per cent of the total cost of educating a student; the remaining 65 per cent of expenses for each student had to be provided from other sources, mostly gifts in kind from private donors. Students on scholarships from the Hariri Foundation constituted 40 per cent of the total student body. I argued that student scholarships should cover the total cost and not just the tuition fee. This form of sponsorship was standard practice at educational institutions worldwide, so it came as a surprise to me that it did not apply at BUC. When I raised this matter with Riyad Nassar, he said that an official request along these lines had been made to the Hariri Foundation, but that they categorically refused to pay more than the basic tuition. The leadership of BUC feared that if they pressed the Hariri Foundation on this point, the Foundation would transfer their students to other universities. I recognised all this but said that if they did agree, the College would be saving a 65 per cent subsidy to cover this shortfall, which is a sizeable amount.

I reluctantly came to the conclusion that we could break out of BUC's funding dilemma only by raising tuition fees by almost threefold to balance the budget. I realised that by doing so, it would make it difficult for families of modest incomes to send their children to BUC. Students who relied on the Hariri Foundation (40 per cent of the student body) could, however, meet the higher tuition fees. Of the non-Hariri students (60 per cent), we estimated that approximately half could afford to pay higher tuition out of their own pockets but that the remaining half would desperately need financial assistance. My three-point plan, drafted in direct talks with President Nassar, included the following measures:

- BUC would increase tuition fees over a period of two years to cover up to 90 per cent of the total cost of educating our students.

- BUC would establish a special fund to provide needy students with up to 35 per cent of their tuition fees.

- As an incentive to the faculty and senior members of the administration, a portion of their salaries would be paid in US dollars at a fixed exchange rate.

The Board approved the plan which, in my opinion, was a major step towards balancing the budget of the college. Having met the immediate short-term crisis, I turned my attention to what I saw as the key long-term issue, namely BUC's lack of a General Endowment Fund.

Riyad mentioned that he had some good news regarding the establishment of an Endowment Fund. The McKune Foundation had offered a generous gift of $1,000,000, payable if BUC could raise $1,500,000 within a one-year period. I assured him that we could raise this sum, and I pledged to make up any shortfall that existed as the deadline approached. I was appointed to head a special emergency fundraising task force, and immediately allocated office space at our London headquarters to support this campaign. The fund received its first infusion of cash from three Board of Trustees members, namely Kamal Shair, Alex Bouri, and myself. We each pledged $60,000, for a total of $180,000. I also reached out to friends and colleagues to solicit financial support. My friends Hasib Sabbagh and Said Khoury responded generously by giving $60,000 each. President Nassar worked with his contacts and BUC's traditional contributors, such as the Ford Foundation and major oil companies. In addition, we mailed thousands upon thousands of letters to alumni and friends of the College asking for contributions.

Our efforts were so fruitful that, by the closing date of our fundraising drive at the end of 1985, we had collected all the necessary money. In fact, we had surpassed expectations by raising $250,000 over the needed $1,500,000. Especially gratifying to me was the fact that contributions by Arab nationals had exceeded contributions by American and other foreign nationals. BUC's General Endowment Fund was now established with a total of nearly $3,000,000. In sum, within a year of my assuming the responsibilities of Chairman of the Board, BUC's financial status was stabilised and steadily improving. The Board praised this achievement and the general atmosphere of the College, in particular the performance of the administration, was greatly enhanced.

*   *   *

Having succeeded in resolving the financial problems, we had to concentrate on the academic standards of the college. BUC was renowned for its high competitive standard since its foundation (originally the Junior College for Women in Beirut) by the Presbyterian Church of New York in 1927. Unfortunately, BUC's standards were inevitably compromised during the war in Lebanon that began in 1975 and which I have described elsewhere. Even more disastrous was the cycle of violence that followed in the wake of the Israeli occupation of Lebanon in 1982. This made it very difficult for a large number of students to commute daily to the campus in Ras Beirut.

To compensate for its troubles, BUC developed a collaborative relationship in the late 1970s with the Order of the Maronite Monks at Louweizi in the north of Beirut. It was agreed that BUC students could take classes at Louweizi and receive credits from BUC. A similar arrangement was made with Al-Makased at Sidon in the south of Beirut. This arrangement, however, did produce administrative and academic difficulties between BUC and its associates at both locations to the extent that following the President's report, the Board had to spend most of its time trying to resolve these problems. Naturally, the situation could not continue like this. A permanent solution was needed; therefore, I suggested that BUC have its own campuses in both locations. A few Board members objected strongly to this suggestion, but the majority kept silent. The President remarked that this would be a very good thing to do but with hardly any funds to keep the existing campus in operation, there was no money to invest in the creation of these new campuses. In any case, such a plan would require an official request from all Board members to be submitted to the Board of Regents for approval.

I had learned since my early days at work not to give up easily. I pressed all Board members to consider my suggestion seriously. Finally, they agreed with the provision that capital investment would not be incurred by the institution in creating these two campuses; it had to be done through gifts in kind by private donors. This was a tremendous challenge, but I accepted it and asked the President to submit this request to the Board of Regents for approval, which was granted, shortly after, in the spring of 1987.

Our decision was announced to the public with a request for land donations for two campuses. Although there were no offers made for the Sidon campus, a subsidiary company of Zakhem International, New Byblos Company (NBC), which owned land on

Social and Philanthropic Work

a hill overlooking the city of Byblos two kilometres away from the seashore, ancient fort, and seaport, made a very tempting offer for this land to be the site for the Byblos campus. The Board accepted the gift of 100,000 square metres of land for the BUC campus at Byblos with many thanks and gratitude, and were appreciative of my contribution in this respect.

We relinquished our relationship with the Order of the Monks at Louweizi, and directly established a branch of BUC at Byblos town until the new campus was officially established. The temporary accommodation was made possible through gifts of two buildings on the periphery of the city. This was made possible by myself and my friend, Alex Bouri – another member of the Board.

News of BUC's new branch at Byblos spread quickly, and caused reactions in certain circles that I found incomprehensible. Two members of the Board of Trustees, for example, were totally against the new campus. More remarkably, faculty and students at BUC's Beirut campus expressed fierce opposition. Those who opposed the creation of a new campus spread all kinds of rumours to discredit the project, such as spurious claims that we were depleting funds from the Beirut campus to pay for Byblos. Demonstrations were staged and hostile articles appeared in newspapers. The situation escalated when opponents of the project received support from media outlets located in west Beirut which were affiliated with armed militias. Some politicians jumped on the 'anti' bandwagon, claiming that I was sponsoring the BUC presence in Byblos (a Christian community) to the detriment and ultimate termination of the BUC campus in Beirut (located in a Muslim community).

Lebanon's Acting Prime Minister, Salim El Hoss, visited London on official business. At a gathering there he said to me: 'I don't believe in dividing education, and your action is divisionary and therefore unacceptable.' Even more surprising, certain dignitaries of the Maronite Church expressed opposition: they did not want an institution inspired by the American model of liberal education operating in a traditional Maronite area. I have never understood to this day why the US embassy in Beirut had to declare its opposition to this project which added to the stream of objections against BUC's Byblos campus.

Girding ourselves against all criticism, we went ahead with our plans and began construction in the spring of 1988. By the end of that year, fighting between warring factions resumed after the outgoing President, Amine Gemayel, appointed General Aoun as Prime Minister. Especially intense was the fighting that raged between the Christian militia 'Lebanese Forces' and army units loyal to General Aoun. This cycle of clashes delayed our construction for at least a year, and the project was not completed until the end of 1990.

* * *

In private conversations with BUC's President, Riyad Nassar, we invariably turned to the subject of transforming the college into a university. On one occasion he said to me: 'In order to comply with Lebanese law, if we want to be a university we need to have four schools instead of our one existing school of Arts and Science. As you know, we also have a combined engineering programme with Georgia Tech University in the US that could be developed on the new campus if space is available. We also have all the facilities to establish a School of Computer Science. This would leave us with one additional school to create from scratch, and I believe we should open a School of Pharmacy.' I agreed wholeheartedly with President Nassar, but also saw wisdom in planning for schools of Medicine and Agriculture as well. I said to him: 'I suggest that we submit an official report on this subject to the Board describing our vision for the future. This report could be in the form of a fifteen-year expansion plan. Consider elaborating in our report the proposed transformation and the development of the three campuses: Beirut, Byblos, and Sidon.'

We did in fact submit a report to the Board in advance of our March 1988 meeting. At that meeting, the Board adopted the report in its entirety with only minor modifications. In my view, the acceptance of the plan constituted a major achievement in the history of BUC. Now we had an organisational plan to develop and operate as a private university with three campuses: one main campus and two branches. The President would have three Vice Presidents: one each for Academic Affairs, Administration and Finance, and Student Affairs. During the first five years, BUC would inaugurate the Byblos campus and apply officially to the government of Lebanon to alter its classification from a college to a university with a new name. During the second five-year period,

Social and Philanthropic Work

the plan envisaged construction of the Sidon campus to accommodate the School of Agriculture and any other schools that the Board chose to establish. The third five-year interval provided for the inauguration of a Medical School at the Byblos campus. By the end of fifteen years, we estimated that our new university would have approximately 10,000 students.

By 1991, the first phase of the plan to transform BUC into a university was almost complete. In October, the new Byblos campus was inaugurated. BUC became known as the Lebanese American University (LAU); along with the new name, it had new by-laws and a new organisational chart. Dr Nabil Haidar was appointed as LAU's Senior Vice President for Academic Affairs. I knew Nabil was highly qualified and that he would fully honour all his obligations. The institution's budget rose from $3,000,000 to around $25,000,000, while student enrolment increased from 3,000 to approximately 4,300. The general endowment fund that was established during my first year as Chairman of the Board approached $50,000,000. As my term as Chairman came to an end, I was satisfied that all I had set out to accomplish had been achieved during my six-year tenure.

As a member of the Board of Trustees, I was very aware of the importance of implementing stages two and three of the fifteen-year plan described earlier. Finding funds for the building programmes at Byblos and Beirut became easier as fundraising gained momentum. The Zakhem firm's donation of an engineering building at LAU's Byblos campus set a precedent for other Lebanese to follow, just as I had hoped it would. Among those who stepped forward with generous support were George Frem and his brother Antoine, Sami Kurban, Francois Baseel, Nehmi Tome, Rizk Rizk, and Mohammed Safadi.

As far as academic disciplines were concerned, LAU's new Pharmacy School was launched, with the expectation that it would be followed by the establishment of a School of Medicine and a School of Agriculture. The School of Agriculture was to open on the Sidon campus, and so it had to await completion of the new buildings at that location. For its part, the Medical School would be located at Byblos, but to open its doors we needed a sizeable amount of funding. Additionally, LAU had to obtain a special government permit to operate a Medical School, which was no easy task.

In March 1993, during a short visit to Houston after the Board of Trustees meeting in New York, I met with my close friend Michel Halbouty at his office. As we spoke about Lebanon and whether or not the general political situation had improved, I shared with him my feelings of despair concerning Lebanon's future. I told him what I believed was a key challenge for the long-term stability of Lebanon: getting the US government to engage in Lebanon in a positive way. I mentioned that I had made a deliberate decision not to involve myself in Lebanese politics directly. Instead, I chose to help my country and people by focusing on higher education. 'As you know, Mike,' I said to Michel Halbouty, 'I've been involved with the Lebanese American University for over ten years and with Balamand University since it was founded six years ago. The Zakhem family has contributed around $10,000,000 to LAU and committed around half that amount to BU. You will be pleased to know that during the LAU Board meeting last week in New York, two resolutions that relate to me personally were adopted: first, choosing a date for the official inauguration of the Zakhem Engineering Building; and second, conferring on me the first Honorary Doctorate Degree given by the university.'

I mentioned that it had always been my intention to honour those Americans of Lebanese origin who excelled in their field, displaying their names on the buildings we were constructing on the Byblos Campus. For example, we decided to name the library building after Gibran Kahlil Gibran.

'I hope we will be able to display your name on one in the future. But what occupies my mind now is how to establish the Medical School and I have been thinking that it would be nice to have Dr Michael DeBakey's name displayed.'

He replied: 'George, I think this is an excellent idea and I am sure that he will accept; of course the best thing to do is to talk to him. I will call him now to request a meeting with you.'

I said, 'Really, you don't have to do it now; on my next visit.'

He said with an asserting voice, 'No, we will do it now.'

He picked up the phone, spoke to Dr DeBakey, and fixed a meeting for the next day at 11:00 a.m. at his office at the Methodist Hospital, Houston Medical Center.

My meeting with Dr DeBakey was overwhelming. I was in the presence of two prominent men of Lebanese origin: Dr Michael

DeBakey and Mr Michel Halbouty. Until his passing, Dr DeBakey was Chancellor Emeritus of the Baylor College of Medicine in Houston, and was internationally recognised as an ingenious medical inventor and innovator, a gifted and dedicated teacher, and an outstanding surgeon. Mr Halbouty is one of the world's foremost geologists and petroleum engineers and is considered an outstanding authority on the geological and engineering challenges of exploring and producing petroleum. Both men were around the same age – in their late eighties – but still remarkably active.

Michel Halbouty began the meeting by addressing Dr DeBakey: 'I've known George Zakhem for over fifteen years, and I know he's one of those few people taking responsibility for his country's future, which is also our country. He has an idea and all I ask of you is to listen to what he has to say and then give him your clear and honest opinion as to whether you agree to it or not.' I then made a brief presentation on the transformation of BUC into LAU. I concluded by noting that one of the final steps in the creation of LAU was launching a Medical College at our Byblos campus. I said that the Board of Trustees and the President of LAU would be honoured if the new Medical College bore the name of Dr Michael DeBakey.

Dr DeBakey responded by saying that he was indeed honoured to receive this request, but he was concerned about the quality and standard of medical education that could be achieved in Lebanon given how the country was only just emerging from decades of turmoil. He proposed that LAU consider an affiliation between its Medical School and the Baylor College of Medicine. I replied, 'I shall ask our Board to adopt your proposal and to follow your recommendation step by step.' At the end of the meeting, we agreed to form a Steering Committee whose members were: Michel Halbouty (distinguished earth scientist, engineer, author, and lecturer); Philip Salem MD (Director of the Cancer Research Program at St Luke's Episcopal Hospital in Houston, and a world-famous oncologist); Nadim Zacca MD (Associate Professor of Cardiology at Baylor Methodist Hospital in Houston); Antoine Zakhem MD; Riyad Nassar; and myself to work with Dr DeBakey and liaise with Baylor College.

I informed Dr Philip Salem and Dr Nadim Zacca of the outcome of my meeting with Dr DeBakey, and they were very pleased and expressed their willingness to do all they could in support of the project. I telephoned Riyad Nassar, who was in Washington, and told him the whole story as well. Riyad was supportive and suggested that the plan be submitted to LAU's Board, and I did so.

During its first meeting, our Steering Committee took three major decisions:

- We decided to approach Baylor and hold a combined meeting to solicit their approval for an association with LAU. Dr DeBakey undertook this responsibility and discussed the subject with President Faigan of Baylor, who showed interest in the project. Meetings were held between representatives of Baylor and LAU, and a Memorandum of Understanding was signed between the two institutions signifying their agreement to cooperate on the creation of the DeBakey Medical Centre at Byblos.

- We decided to hire a Texas-based firm of architects with experience in the design of similar facilities. This firm would prepare a preliminary study and cost estimate. The services of Hamilton, Watson & Associates were retained for this purpose.

- We decided to arrange a visit by Dr DeBakey to LAU facilities in Beirut and Byblos as soon as the security situation in Lebanon allowed us to do so.

The implementation of these decisions required funding to the amount of $250,000, which I pledged would be paid by the Zakhem company. The architects were commissioned and completed their study within three months. Dr DeBakey made his journey to Lebanon during the second week of November 1994 along with his wife, Katrine. Philip Salem and Nadim Zacca, my brother Antoine, my wife Lisa, and myself accompanied them on a private, chartered aeroplane from London to Beirut. During his visit to Lebanon, Dr DeBakey was hailed by the media and was warmly welcomed at the presidential palace by the President of the Republic, Elias Hrawi. President Hrawi bestowed on his guest the Shield of Honour of the Cedars of Lebanon, one of Lebanon's highest decorations. Dr DeBakey also met with Prime Minister Rafic Hariri, Speaker of Parliament Nabih Berri, and Foreign Minister Faris Bouweiz. His visits to the Beirut city centre, as well as other cities such as Byblos

Social and Philanthropic Work

and Ba'albeck, revived memories of his early years when, at the age of eight, he spent six months in Lebanon. Above all, he was touched by the reception he received in the City Café, Hamra, where he met members of the Dabaghy (DeBakey) family who had come all the way from his hometown village of Marjeioun in the far south in order to greet him.

Dr DeBakey's visit was a success in all respects. Most importantly, it bestowed momentum on the effort to establish a medical college at Byblos. Despite progress on this important project, a few members of the LAU Board, as well as some LAU faculty, objected to the Medical School. To my great surprise, three institutions that already had Medical Schools in operation – AUB, St Joseph, and the Lebanese University – let their opposition be known. The Association of Lebanese Doctors and some members of Parliament also shared their negative views of what we were trying to do.

To allay concerns about the expense associated with creating a Medical School, we launched a special fund that would solicit gifts from private donors. Immediately, the Michael DeBakey Foundation pledged $500,000 and I matched this amount on behalf of the Zakhem company. The Board authorised construction to begin once the special fund totalled $15,000,000. The Board agreed that half of this amount would be earmarked from the university's general fund to be paid over a three-year period. This left $7,500,000 to be raised from private sources, of which one million had been secured. Our goal was to raise the additional $6,500,000 over the next three years.

As matters developed, fundraising was not our primary problem, for it took no less than six years for LAU to receive the necessary permit from the government of Lebanon. Thanks to lobbying by Dr DeBakey and the influence of the Minister of Higher Education at the time, Mohammed Y. Beydoun, the permit was finally obtained in 2000. The delay in this process, however, was fatal as it allowed the forces of opposition to rally and re-group. Alas, by August 2005, LAU had a new President but no new Medical Centre. In the final analysis, an outstanding opportunity had been lost, and this was a tragedy not only for LAU but also for Lebanon as a whole.

The failure in establishing the Medical School at LAU, then, was amply compensated by the success of Balamand University (BU) in obtaining a government permit for their school at the same time.

In October 2000, the Medical School at BU admitted its first students who eventually graduated as fully qualified doctors in June 2005. As a Trustee on the Board of Balamand University, I am proud of BU's achievement. Presently, I am working to establish the DeBakey Chair of Cardiovascular and Heart Surgery at BU's Medical School.

* * *

In 2002, my interest in working on behalf of LAU started to wane when I discovered that certain members of the Board were manoeuvring to prevent the Senior Vice President for Academic Affairs, Nabil Haidar, from succeeding the retiring President, Riyad Nassar. Over the years, I saw first-hand how Nabil worked tirelessly on behalf of BUC/LAU and I was convinced that he was the best candidate to take the helm of the institution. But faculty members who were envious of Nabil swayed other members of the Board – who were also envious of me. As the question of succession was debated within the Board, a serious split developed. This disagreement filtered out into the LAU community and even into the media. Proposals to break the impasse were made by representatives of the Synod of the Presbyterian Church of Lebanon and Syria, but these were rejected. I made a proposal to safeguard the interests of LAU, but it was not even entertained by the Board. As a result, I decided that I could do no more for LAU and announced my resignation as Trustee.

After I left the LAU Board, the remaining members extended the contract of President Riyad Nassar for two years. In 2003, it was announced that Dr Joseph Jabbra would take over as the next President of LAU the following year. After his contract was extended, Riyad Nassar's first act was to discharge Nabil Haidar who had served the university with total diligence for thirty-two years. Fortunately, Nabil was immediately hired by the American University of Science and Technology (AUST) in Beirut to serve as its Provost. Needless to say, I was totally frustrated by this turn of events.

* * *

His Beatitude Ignatius IV, Patriarch of the Greek Orthodox Church for Antioch and the Orient – my church – made his first visit to Western Europe in May 1983. I was a member of the party that met him at the VIP lounge of Heathrow airport. Other members of the welcoming delegation included Lebanon's Ambassador to the UK and Ireland, General Ahmed Al Haj, and the Ambassador of Syria. I was the Chairman of the Antiochian Orthodox Society of Britain and had just concluded an agreement with the Archdeacon of London under which the Anglican Church leased one of their churches to serve our parish.

The Patriarch is the head of our church and in that capacity presides over meetings of the Counsel of the Metropolites (Archbishops), which meets twice a year at his headquarters in Damascus. There are now twenty Metropolites in the Church of Antioch, six in Lebanon, five in Syria, one in Iraq-Kuwait, six in the Americas, one in Western Europe, and one in Australia. Each Metropolite has jurisdiction over his own monasteries and churches in his area of responsibility. The same applies to the Patriarch, who has jurisdiction over a number of monasteries spread over various countries.

At the end of the Patriarch's visit to London, he called for a meeting in Geneva to be attended by selected members of our church who resided in Western Europe. The Patriarch asked me to attend, and I did so with around twenty other persons. At the meeting, various subjects were discussed and two major decisions were taken. First, an Economic and Development Advisory Board was formed to assist His Beatitude with securing additional funding for projects supported by the Greek Orthodox Church for Antioch and the Orient. Second, it was decided to build an Orthodox Centre with guest quarters in the suburbs of Beirut. Metropolite Khodre allocated land for this project at Mansouriya, a mountain suburb east of Beirut. Money to cover construction costs would have to be raised from members of our congregation. Five of us pledged one million Lebanese pounds ($250,000) each, and four others pledged half a million each. With 70 per cent of the needed money raised, we thought the project was viable. His Beatitude was pleased with the outcome of the meeting and thanked everyone for making generous contributions of time and money.

Back in Lebanon, however, war was raging and was particularly intense in the areas around Mansouriya, the very location we had chosen for the proposed Orthodox Centre. Options were discussed for relocating the new Orthodox Centre, perhaps to a villa in the Sin El-Fil area of Beirut, but no final decision was taken.

Meanwhile, Patriarch Ignatius made a second visit to Europe in 1985. In conjunction with this trip, the Economic and Development Advisory Board met in Paris. The most important item on the agenda was securing funding for the Balamand School of Theology (which had some fifty students) and the Balamand High School (which had a roll of around 400 students). At this time, we were all deeply concerned because approximately 150,000 of our church members had been displaced by the war from their villages in the mountains around Beirut and the south to safer areas north of the city. In all wars the problem of accommodating displaced people is extremely complex. Even now Lebanon is still struggling with how to resolve this issue once and for all.

While the members of the Patriarch's Economic and Development Advisory Board debated how to deal with our community's immediate crises, I was more interested in the future and how to deal with long-term issues. It occurred to me that someday – hopefully sooner rather than later – the war in Lebanon would end. In peacetime, nothing would be needed more than to educate the young people of our war-ravaged country, so why not found a university at Balamand sponsored by the Orthodox Church? The other religious communities of Lebanon were already in a position to contribute to the education of the Lebanese people. The Presbyterians sponsored AUB and later LAU, the Maronites have St Joseph, and the Muslims run al-Makased and the Arab University. Furthermore, many of Lebanon's most distinguished professors and thinkers hailed from the Orthodox community, including Constantine Zurayek, Charles Malik who had played a pivotal role in founding the UN, Nicola Shahine, Nazih Taleb, Mousa Ghantous, Adib Sarkis, Afif Moufarrej, Nicola Ziadeh, and Mikhail Naimy – perhaps the most well-known man of letters who wrote in both English and Arabic.

* * *

Having thought carefully about the concept of founding a new university, I put my thoughts down on paper and submitted this document the next day to His Beatitude and my fellow Board members. I gave a simple explanation of the reasons that led me to make the proposal and left it to them to take the appropriate decision. After I finished speaking, I was surprised to see that nobody had any reaction whatsoever, except to look in the direction of the Patriarch for his comments. The Patriarch declined to comment and we turned to other items on the agenda. In fact, my proposal was not even referred to in the minutes of the meeting. I was somewhat disappointed but decided not to pursue the matter further.

I could not keep my counsel for long, however, because I have been trained to say what I believe openly and without fear. In Paris, I shared my discontent with Bishop Saliby, who was subsequently appointed as Metropolite of the Antiochian Orthodox Church of Western Europe. I did the same with other members of our community when I returned to London. Bishop Saliby passed my remarks on to the Patriarch.

After a year and a half I met with my friend Samir Khairallah in London, a famous architect who had been commissioned to prepare the master plan for LAU's Byblos campus. During our talk Samir told me that he had recently met with His Beatitude Ignatius IV in Damascus. Samir said 'I have a message for you from his Beatitude Ignatius which I should deliver; he is visiting Geneva in early January and would like to meet with you there to discuss the university project at Balamand. I think you should go and meet him.' I hesitated but I agreed to go to Geneva, and in the course of discussions with His Beatitude it was decided that a university located on the grounds of the Monastery of Balamand would be founded with the name Balamand University. To assist in this great task, a Board of Trustees would be formed consisting of Atef Daniel, Abdallah Tamari, William Kazan, Ghassan Tueini, Elie Salem, Adib Sarkis, Saeid Khoury, and others. Candidates for the position of university President were also discussed.

As always, funding the construction of new buildings was a key problem, but we were sure that a group of wealthy individuals would contribute gifts in kind towards our noble and important project. I pledged to His Beatitude that the Zakhem family would be among the first contributors and that we would be honoured to have a building on the new campus named after my father and mother.

Upon returning to Beirut, the Patriarch allocated land for the new campus, registered the university's name with the proper authorities, and appointed members of the Board. A few months later, His Beatitude stopped in London for two days on his way to the United States. I met with him at his hotel and was briefed on the progress of Balamand University (BU). With His Beatitude was BU's contractor, my friend Elias Abu Shahin. Elias explained the plan of the campus, which was to have a cloister of small buildings with a few entrances surrounding a common atrium. I learned that construction was proceeding apace. The cost of each building varied between $700,000 and $1,000,000.

Frankly, I was disappointed by the building plan for BU and said to His Beatitude: 'This is below the standard of buildings I would recommend for the campus. We had agreed in our meeting in Geneva to appoint a firm of architects and town planners to prepare a master plan for the whole site and I do not see that this was done.' Both His Beatitude and Elias responded that construction had already begun and so it was not possible to change course now. I could see that there was no possibility of altering this decision and remained quiet despite my acute disappointment with the plans I had seen. After the meeting, I was not briefed again on the progress of the construction. In fact, I could follow matters only by reading Lebanese newspapers. Eventually, Dr George Tohmeh was appointed as President of BU. Towards the end of 1988 I had an opportunity to speak with him during a meeting in Paris with His Beatitude and a few Board members. Because of Dr Tohmeh's age and poor health, it was obvious that he would be incapable of serving effectively as President. I knew I could do nothing to change the appointment, so I kept my thoughts to myself. A year later, Ghassan Tueini – a former Minister and Ambassador to the UN who was also Editor of the prestigious newspaper *Annahar* – replaced Dr Tohmeh.

Ghassan Tueini is an extremely capable fellow, but it was clear to me that he was not the right person to serve as BU's President. The institution was still very much in its formative stage and would require the total attention of its Chief Executive. Ghassan had too many other competing interests making demands on his time and attention. Furthermore, as a politician he was highly opinionated and could not detach himself from politics to focus on building a university. Let me emphasise that my opposition to Ghassan in no way means I lack respect for him. In fact, I have such great esteem for Ghassan that I have for many years urged him to write his memoirs so that this and future generations of Lebanese can benefit from his wisdom. I am acutely aware of what we all lose when important figures pass away without leaving a written legacy. For example, the great Lebanese Dr Charles Malik and Emile Bustani both died without writing their memoirs.

As I feared, BU had not completely fulfilled its great potential. Ghassan divided his time between BU, *Annahar*, and his political interests. Inevitably, he delegated many of his duties at BU to subordinates, a poor model of leadership under any circumstances. BU admitted its first students in 1988, all of whom graduated in 1991, but I was not satisfied with the standard of education the students were receiving. Similarly, I was not satisfied with the way BU's buildings were constructed and how the campus layout was shaped. To my mind, a university is meant to serve future generations by giving them the best possible education. After much thought, I decided to remain silent, and remembered the Arabic saying: 'If spoken words were of silver, then silence is of gold.'

But after two years of boycotting Board meetings, I felt it was wrong; I should attend and give my opinion about the affairs of the university to his Beatitude and all the members. So I decided to attend a meeting of BU's Board that was to be held on the university campus in early July 1993. Also in attendance were the Chairman of the Board Patriarch Ignatius IV, the President of the university Ghassan Tueini, most Board members, and senior members of the faculty. At the appropriate moment, I made it clear that the university needed a new President with proven experience in academic affairs, one with a doctoral degree who could dedicate himself *full-time* to managing the affairs of the institution. I said that despite his undeniable eminence, Ghassan Tueini was not the right man for the position, not least because he could not detach himself from politics. I said that the matter was very urgent and that an emergency search committee had to be formed to find a new President to succeed Ghassan Tueini.

I knew that my remarks would make me some enemies, but a majority of Board members endorsed my views, albeit privately after the formal meeting adjourned. His Beatitude listened to me attentively and made only one comment: 'We are here to listen to suggestions anyone may have.' Understandably, Ghassan was furious at my suggestion. He lit a cigarette and walked out of the room with an expression of disgust. He came back later and addressed the group, his eyes focused squarely on the Patriarch: 'I'm here doing this job voluntarily,' he said. 'I donate my salary to BU. Your Beatitude, please kindly relieve me of my duties as soon as possible.' He went on to say, 'I know where Mr Zakhem is coming from. He owes allegiance to LAU.'

Two weeks later I received a copy of the minutes of the meeting. They did not include the remarks I had made. Immediately I wrote to His Beatitude and President Tueini asking for the minutes to be amended to reflect my comments. Understandably, Ghassan took my statements as a personal rebuke and so a certain ill feeling overshadowed our personal relations. I was able to clear the air during a meeting with him at his office in Beirut. On that occasion, I assured him that my conclusions were not directed against him or anyone else. I told him, 'The best service we can offer to BU and His Beatitude is to assist in finding a person with the right qualifications who, as President, will dedicate himself to the university on a full-time basis.' 'Alright,' Ghassan responded, 'I've already submitted my resignation but will carry on with the search for the new President and will be in contact with you.' About a month later, I received a telephone call from Ghassan. He told me that they had reviewed a list of names and had determined that the best candidate for the presidency of BU was Dr Elie Salem. If I agreed with this selection, then His Beatitude would propose Elie to the Board of Trustees at their next meeting. I replied that I fully agreed with the nomination.

The Board met the following month and voted to appoint Elie Salem as the next President of BU. Elie was, in fact, always my first choice to be President. When BU was launched in 1987, however, he was serving as Senior Foreign Policy Advisor to Lebanon's President, Amine Gemayel, after having served as Foreign Minister of Lebanon during the first phase of the Gemayel presidency. After the end of President Gemayel's term in 1988, Elie had returned to his private academic life. There was no doubt in my mind that he was the man who could save BU, but I reminded him that this would only be possible if he did not get involved in politics in any shape or form.

In one of our private conversations, His Beatitude asked when construction of the building sponsored by our family would commence. I replied that we would begin construction as soon as the location for the building had been selected. He suggested that

Social and Philanthropic Work

I discuss the matter with BU's new President. Elie Salem and I selected the site on campus for the building and my friend, Toni Khoury, was commissioned to do the architectural design. A few years later the building was completed and duly inaugurated in January 2005 and named after my parents, Salim and Hanneh Zakhem. The architecture of the building was inspired by the structure and stonework of the Monastery of Balamand. The building features three floors, a 500-seat auditorium, a banquet hall, a café, an infirmary, and various halls for student activities. It was designed to look like a shrine which not only enhances the spiritual atmosphere of the building, but also adds significantly to the beauty of BU's campus.

Elie did not disappoint those of us who believed that BU was in need of a major overhaul. Immediately after assuming office, he instituted important reforms to the university's academic, administrative, and development programmes. In less than two years, BU's new President gained the respect and admiration of the entire Board of Trustees and, even more importantly, of His Beatitude Ignatius IV. Among the highlights of Elie's tenure are the following accomplishments: commissioning a campus master plan that specifies future building and landscaping; opening a Medical School; creating a plan to integrate the Académie des Beaux Arts in Beirut into BU; creating an Engineering department to supervise campus construction projects; organising and founding the BU Alumni Association; and launching the Dr Michael DeBakey Chair of Cardiovascular and Heart Surgery at BU's Medical School.

Today, Elie Salem continues to lead BU with distinction, and I do everything possible to assist him in his efforts. In 1995, he and His Beatitude Ignatius IV visited London and I organised a special dinner at The Dorchester in their honour. At this function, I was honoured to receive the Golden Cross of St Peter and St Paul from His Beatitude in appreciation of my work on behalf of BU. I was humbled and pleased by this decoration and promised to continue to serve BU as long as I live.

I have not forgotten my alma mater, AUB, which gave me the opportunity to receive a first-rate education. In June 2005 I visited the Engineering School to receive a special lifetime achievement award. After the celebration and the speeches, I had a meeting with the President of AUB. As a result, my brothers Antoine and Abdallah and I decided to pledge $3,000,000 to establish a deanship of the School of Engineering, which was named the Zakhem Dean of Engineering.

By the year 2005, we had contributed over $18,000,000 to institutions of higher education in Lebanon. This is a figure I believe was only matched by the late Prime Minister Rafic Hariri. Although many of our countrymen have amassed great fortunes and are much wealthier than we are, they have failed to make similar contributions to promote education in our country. I am a believer in what Kahlil Gibran said in his masterpiece, *The Prophet*:

> There are those who give little of the much they have – and they give it for recognition and their hidden desire makes their gift unwholesome. And there are those who have little and give it all. These are the believers in life and the bounty of life, and their coffer is never empty. There are those who give with joy, and that joy is their reward.

I consider myself to be of those who give with joy; therefore, I am content to be rewarded with joy. On Commencement Day for the graduates of the year, I watch those young men and women walking down the aisle, over 2,000 of them from LAU and BU, with pride, pleasure, and total satisfaction. I tell myself, 'Look, George, at the results of your commitment and hard work for these two universities. Certainly, you must be overwhelmed with joy.'

CHAPTER 12

Towards Retirement

In 2000, I turned sixty-five: retirement territory. The world also reached a milestone in that it was the beginning of a new millennium. Various countries marked the occasion in different ways. Some spent millions of dollars to erect special monuments to commemorate the occasion. The media covered celebratory events extensively. Special books were published recalling the past century or speculating about the future. More threatening stories circulated widely about the 'millennium bug' that would disable computer systems worldwide and create chaos. These predictions of doom, of course, never materialised. For me personally, reaching retirement age did not have any influence on my life. I continued to work just as hard as before and, in fact, during that year I was busier than ever.

Around that time our projects in Lebanon were losing tens of millions of dollars. The Riviera Hotel was incurring a loss for the simple reason that more and better hotels opened for business such as the Phoenicia Intercontinental and Vendome. The economy of the country never picked up and visitors to Lebanon did not increase over the years. Our beach hotel at Mombasa was also losing money, mainly because of the threat of terrorism in Kenya that had a negative effect on the number of tourists visiting the country. This hotel could not honour its debts to two major banks, International Finance Corporation (IFC) and Industrial Development Bank (IDB), and both served us with an official notice stating that we had to pay the principle and service charges in full. As a result, major decisions had to be taken and implemented to resolve the situation. We liquidated prime assets in Lebanon and abroad to obtain cash. For example, we sold our interest in three hotels on the Costa Del Sol, Spain: the Marbella Club, the Puente Romano, and the Torrequebrada. Similarly, we sold our interest in the Copthorne Slough-Windsor Hotel in the UK and some other properties in Arlington and Houston, Texas. We also entered into secret negotiations to sell our bank in Lebanon, Allied Business Bank.

On a personal level, I was experiencing heavy pressure to solve our company's problems. To do so, I had to provide cash to cover shortfalls and pay debts. Most importantly, I realised that the company could not be rescued by liquidating assets only; we also needed to secure new and profitable construction projects.

By 1999, we decided to wind down our construction operations in Lebanon. Our operations in Kenya and Tanzania were at a standstill, with minimal prospects for sizeable contracts on the horizon. Surveying our options, I judged that Nigeria offered us growth potential because it had a vibrant construction market, and so we concentrated our efforts in that country. Our biggest hurdle in Nigeria was how to qualify to obtain contracts with the foreign oil companies operating there, including Shell, Chevron, and Agip. After consulting with our Area Manager, Wadie Ghabriel, and a few friends with experience in Nigeria, we decided to partner with a local Nigerian company. We believed that such a partnership would enhance and strengthen our appeal to international oil companies, who favoured doing business with local companies. In 1998, we partnered with Oilserv Limited for one project, and in 2000 we obtained a major contract with Shell to rehabilitate their Bonny Island Terminal. The project was originally valued at $60,000,000 and eventually increased by more than 65 per cent. Around the same time, we secured an EPC (engineering, procurement and construction) contract to construct a 30-inch gas pipeline in Qatar for the Qatar Petroleum Company. In sum, by late 2000 our company was back on track with major contracts in hand.

My brother Albert was posted back to Nigeria to take over the area from Wadie Ghabriel who wanted to retire after working for more than thirty-six years with the company. Prices of oil started to increase after the coalition forces invaded Iraq. By 2005 it had doubled in value at a price of $50 a barrel. As of 2008 it reached as high as $147 a barrel. Translated on the ground this meant a huge increase in the income of oil producing countries. Being one of them, Nigeria embarked on an extensive development programme for its infrastructure and oil and gas resources.

As I had hoped, our operations in Nigeria gained momentum and with Albert at the helm, we were able to secure lucrative contracts from NNPC. Between 2003 and 2007 the company witnessed a remarkable improvement in terms of growth, turnover, and profits. In 2005, for example, the company secured the largest contract from NGC (Nigeria Gas Company): an EPC contract for laying a 36-inch gas pipeline 200 kilometres long. As a result of our success, in 2008 we were awarded two other pipeline projects that exceeded $600,000,000 in value. We had to then increase our staff and mobilise our construction equipment significantly. I was especially pleased that John Derbyshire, one of our senior managers who left the company in 1997, returned as our General Manager in Nigeria. Albert now had more time for expanding our business in other countries in Africa.

* * *

An occasion in February 2001 brought much happiness and joy to my wife Lisa and myself: we were invited for a two-day visit to the Vatican to attend a special Mass dedicated to world peace by his Holiness Pope John Paul II. The Mass was to be held at the Chiesa del Santissimo Nome di Gesù all'Argentina, a church in the heart of Rome. Representatives from several Christian churches had been invited to attend the Mass. My wife and I attended as members of the Antiochian Orthodox Church of Western Europe.

On arrival at the airport in Rome, we were met by a representative of the Vatican and taken to a private car waiting outside. We were escorted by two traffic wardens on their motorcycles who led the way to the Guest House inside the Vatican. Among the guests were notable dignitaries such as the Archbishop of the Church of England, Dr Carey, as well as a number of Bishops from the Greek and Russian Orthodox churches. The following morning, we were driven in private vehicles to the Chiesa del Gesù and were ushered to our reserved seats. His Holiness arrived with his entourage of senior Archbishops. They walked down the aisle to the altar as religious music filled the air. The Pope blessed the congregation and began the Mass. Every Archbishop or Bishop who was seated at the altar stood up and read in his own language the message of peace from the Bible. Metropolite Gabriel Saliby read the same message in Arabic.

After the Mass, sixty of the guests in attendance were invited to have lunch with His Holiness the Pope. My wife Lisa and I were included in this group, and were seated at a table adjacent to the seat of His Holiness. After lunch, we were invited to meet briefly with His Holiness who received us graciously and with great warmth. We were also honoured to pay our respects and receive his blessings.

Overall, it was a very moving experience for Lisa and myself, and it gave us renewed hope at the start of the new millennium.

During a visit to Paris in 2001, I was introduced to the President of Senegal, Abdoulaye Wade, by a close friend. During our meeting, I briefly described our company and offered our services to Senegal. President Wade asked me to visit Dakar as soon as possible to survey, at first hand, prospective projects. I made such a visit a few months later and had the opportunity to meet the President again at his residence for lunch. I was given a guided tour around Dakar and was introduced to government ministers who described Senegal's construction goals under its five-year plan. One project in particular was of great importance to President Wade, namely the construction of a new university: Université pour la Future Afrique (UFA). President Wade, I learned, is a great believer in higher education and he envisioned UFA as an institution that would serve students from countries throughout West Africa. I told the President of my own interest in higher education and expressed my hope that Zakhem International would undertake the construction of this important project.

After returning to London, I briefed my son Marwan on my visit and asked him to visit Senegal to launch a local company. Marwan made his first fact-finding visit shortly thereafter and met with senior officials in various government ministries. Based on his findings, he selected a few projects for which we would compete. One project, construction of the Université pour la Future Afrique, was on our list and we decided to give it top priority. Marwan pursued our plan and secured the contract a few months later. In 2001, he moved from Houston to Dakar to establish our offices, mobilise staff and resources, and start work on the project. In the years that followed, we secured other major contracts in Senegal, including roads and buildings.

In my opinion, there are significant similarities between Beirut and Dakar. Both Lebanon and Senegal were under French mandate, and both countries adopted French as their second language. The people of these two countries have much in common, whether it is in the social life they live, the food they eat, or the sports they play.

Resemblance between Beirut and Dakar is especially striking in terms of their geographical features. Both cities are like peninsulas, one protruding into the Mediterranean Sea and the other into the Atlantic Ocean. In both places, the ground can rise up to 30 metres above sea level and can sink down to zero. The climate is also comparable, with Dakar being warmer by about 8°C throughout the year compared to Beirut.

In 2002 IMEG (International Mechanical Engineering Group), a reputable consulting engineering firm known to me for some thirty years, experienced problems similar to those that had threatened Penspen. The representatives of IMEG contacted me and solicited my assistance. In turn, I called my friend Hani Hakim, owner of ACE (Associated Consulting Engineers), a highly regarded engineering company, and asked if he had any interest in acquiring IMEG. He said he would consider the idea, and so I immediately arranged a meeting in London between IMEG representatives and Hani Hakim. Negotiations between the two parties went on for a few months before a final agreement was concluded under which ACE acquired IMEG. Shortly after, we recruited IMEG as our consulting engineers on the BOST (Bulk Oil Strategic Storage) project in Ghana.

During my first visit to Ghana it was clear to me that the country was the most stable on the West African coast and was, therefore, poised to play a leading role in the region. Although Ghana's oil reserves have not yet been explored, it is rich in other natural resources such as gold, minerals, timber, and cocoa. The country has great potential for economic growth, provided that pro-market reforms are in place and income taxes are not excessive. In my opinion, the sectors of the Ghanaian economy that can certainly attract foreign investment include tourism, and possibly high-tech industries. With the recent discovery of offshore oil, the country's geography and political stability also make it an ideal site for bulk oil storage and downstream operations for export. In addition, many Ghanaians are well educated and highly trained in many fields, including information technology. In sum, Ghana has the potential to become like Singapore in Asia, Dubai in the Gulf, and Rotterdam in Europe.

Meanwhile, the winding down of our businesses in Lebanon kept Abdallah fully occupied. By 2001, we had completed and handed over to the government all the projects in hand. Nevertheless, payments were not forthcoming, and we had to go to court. At the same time, Abdallah was handling the sale of the Allied Business Bank to Group Mediterrané, but this deal was also taking time to conclude. Abdallah is the only person who could stay on top of, and resolve, these issues but I remained in close touch with him and we exchanged ideas about how to proceed at each critical point. In Beirut we found ourselves surrounded by lawyers and mired in court procedures, which is always a waste of time, effort, and money.

In February 2004, Peter Buckley called me from Accra to enquire if we were interested in working in Ghana to construct an oil storage depot for BOST. I have known Peter for over thirty years; we first met in Doha, Qatar, in 1972. Having done business together in Qatar and other countries including Kenya and Nigeria, we became close friends. When Peter became the CEO of Penspen, their engineering company in London, we remained in close contact. During the early 1990s, the founder of Penspen passed away and the remaining partners differed on policy and strategy. Peter consulted with me and asked if I might be interested in taking over the company. I declined because I thought that it would create a conflict of interest with our business, as they are consultants and we are contractors. I did, however, put Peter in touch with a friend of mine, Dr Kamal Shair, owner and Chairman of the engineering firm Dar Al Handasa. Peter and Kamal met in London and began negotiating an arrangement. Nine months later a deal was concluded whereby Dar Al Handasa took over Penspen. A new board, with Kamal as Chairman, was formed and Peter remained as CEO.

All went well for seven years, after which time Peter decided to leave Penspen to work as an independent consultant. In January 2003, he was retained by BOST Ghana to act as their advisor on their new project for a strategic bulk storage facility. During his first visit to Accra, he learned that they needed the services of specialised contractors for the job, so he immediately contacted me. Of course, I was interested in the project and deputed my son Marwan to visit Accra and meet with Peter and BOST. He did and in July 2004, after four months of pre-tendering and post-tendering negotiations against international competitors such as Entrepose of France, we were awarded the project. This was the shortest time spent to secure a contract and a record in the history of the company.

As a direct result of our success on the BOST project, in early 2005 we were awarded contracts to build two other depots in different locations in Ghana.

*   *   *

Our Lebanon situation weighed heavily on our company and on me personally since I had to carry the financial burden and provide money from other areas of work to cover our Lebanese losses. Finally our financial situation started to improve due to the simple fact that the revenue from our projects in Ghana and Nigeria generated excess cash. In addition we achieved an out-of-court settlement on one project with the government of Lebanon that was completed and handed over four years earlier. Also, we obtained an interim payment from Group Mediterrané for the purchase of the Allied Business Bank. This payment was the result of an Arbitration Board ruling presided over by H. E. Fuad Boutros as umpire. In spite of the ruling in February 2004 by the Arbitration Board, the Chairman of Mediterrané Group refused to pay. We submitted our claim to the Prime Minister at the time who was also the owner of the Group, but he did not overrule the Chairman. Having no other alternatives, we resorted to settling the matter in court and finally were awarded our money on December 28th 2004. The Chairman of the Mediterrané Group was acquitted by the owner directly thereafter.

As busy as Abdallah was extricating our company from our Lebanese entanglements, he was constantly on the lookout for new ventures in the Gulf and North Africa. In 2003, Abdallah concluded a breakthrough deal in Algeria, where he secured a mining concession at the Tarana gold mine. The concession comprised two phases: first, to conduct a site survey and prepare a feasibility study; and second, to develop the mine and extract ore, with proceeds divided between the government of Algeria and Zakhem International. The feasibility study was completed by late 2004, and since 2005 we have been exploring the most economical way to execute phase two.

Mining is a new venture for Zakhem International, and may prove to be a lucrative alternative to our traditional operations in construction. We face major decisions regarding the Algerian mine concession, such as whether to make considerable capital expenditures on our own or share them with investment partners. Another alternative is to sell the concession to a third party.

Having been introduced to the Algerian market, we were able to secure the first pipeline contract for a 48-inch gas pipeline from Sonatrac in 2005. This was followed by a water supply contract in 2007. In both cases we formed consortiums with two other local companies, Cosider and Kanagas, to execute the projects.

Given the wide-ranging operations of Zakhem International in many countries and fields of endeavour, I am still actively involved in the business. In fact, as Chairman of the Board, I still aspire to achieve two main goals before I retire. First, I want to develop and expand our business even further. Second, I would like to see the second generation of Zakhems become well entrenched in the management of the company.

To date, I am very pleased with how matters have developed with Zakhem International, and I feel very much at ease now. In the past five years, our business has entered four African countries: Senegal, Ghana, Algeria, and the Republic of Congo (Congo-Brazzaville). Good prospects for expansion exist in all four countries. In the last two years, 2007 and 2008, we were able to make a breakthrough in the field of power generation. We have embarked on contracts to build two new power stations in Ghana and Congo-Brazzaville. We have also secured other contracts; for example, to build an extension to the airport terminal in Dakar, as well as regulating and metering stations for the West African Gas Pipeline (WAGP) in Ghana, Benin, and Togo. The WAGP will transport natural gas from Nigeria to Ghana and is sponsored by Chevron. With Cosider we were awarded one of the largest water distribution projects in Algeria.

Our strong belief in Ghana, its economy, and the tenacity of its people prompted us to undertake a very daring and challenging project in Ghana: to develop part of downtown Accra. This project comprises of building around 700,000 square metres on 37 acres of land in the centre of the capital city of Ghana. It will include a five-star hotel, offices, residential buildings and a commercial centre. The hotel building is our first priority and we have agreed with Kempinski International to operate and manage the hotel on completion. We have appointed PSP Engineering and Consulting from Houston, Texas, to do the engineering and Termes Partnership LLP represented by Mr Wadih Hanna to be our financial consultants. Kennedys Solicitors acted on our behalf as legal advisors during the negotiation with the government on terms and conditions. Finally, after two years of negotiations, a contract was signed whereby our subsidiary company, Cascade, will provide the required financing to develop the project against a 50-year lease given by the government. Work is now in progress on the hotel project and is expected to be completed by the middle of 2010.

Our yearly turnover is now in the hundreds of millions of dollars and our orders on the books exceed one billion dollars. Our second-generation management – led by my youngest brother Albert and my two sons, Salim and Marwan – has spearheaded our growth. Albert joined the company in 1979, and over the past five years he has supervised our operations in Nigeria where our revenues have increased threefold. Salim, who joined in 1995, looks after our US interests. He has achieved major strides running his ISP that now generates sizeable income for the group. Marwan, who also joined in 1995, is in charge of our operations in Senegal and Ghana, which have been very successful. In sum, Albert, Salim, and Marwan have individually and collectively improved the Zakhem group's performance. They have introduced important internal reforms that have streamlined operations, boosted efficiency, and enhanced profits.

Because of their successes I feel I can plan my retirement after fifty-three years of service. I am able to take on fewer responsibilities and enormously reduce my duties as Chairman Emeritus of Zakhem International. Throughout my working life so far I have had an average of five and a half hours of sleep a night. To this day, I try to be the first employee on duty whether in the main office or on a construction site. It has become a tradition if not a habit. It is not easy to switch off and just stop work when your mind and body are so active for so long.

Recently, in 2006, I was having coffee with a friend in the early morning at a newly opened coffee house, Le Pain Quotidien, at South Kensington close to our office. I was highly impressed by the whole concept to the extent that I thought it would be suitable to introduce it to the Houston market where my son Salim is working and living. I immediately enquired from the manager if that was possible and he said that it is originally a Belgian bakery-restaurant, and that I would have to contact its headquarters in New York. I did just that and discovered that there are already plans for the US market but other locations would be entertained. When I asked where, the answer was Spain and Portugal. I passed this information to Salim and told him to arrange a meeting in New York to discuss the possibilities. I was convinced that this formula would work in Spain and if he was of the same opinion we should take the franchise without delay. Fortunately, Marwan had made a business friend in Madrid who showed interest in this plan. Action along these lines was taken and in December 2008 the first Le Pain Quotidien restaurant opened its doors to customers in one of the most prestigious streets of Madrid. The second restaurant will open in March 2009, and the third is scheduled for September of the same year. The plan is to open ten restaurants in five years, and thirty in fifteen years located in different towns and cities throughout Spain.

I have worked hard to build our company and sustain it over many years. Now I look forward with great excitement and much hope to have some time to spend on myself. In 2008, we were blessed by the birth of our first grandchild Chloe, a daughter to my son Salim and his wife Fay. Chloe has brought so much joy and happiness to our lives that I am eager to spend more time with her. One of our Lebanese proverbs says: 'More dear than one's children are the grandchildren'. How true this is, for the greatest satisfaction in my life is when I spend time with my granddaughter. I hope that my son Marwan will also find happiness with a loving wife and that God will bless him with children, and bless us – his parents – with more grandchildren.

For the last three decades, I tried to help the educational system in Lebanon in a variety of ways. I did so because I believe that education is the best cure for the ills of society. I hear and read many things about the funds donated by philanthropists to prevent or eradicate certain diseases such as AIDS. It may be good momentarily, but in the long run giving the young generation the proper education is the only cure. Education will also put an end to tyranny and civil wars that are the source of all human suffering in the world. Perhaps now I will have some time to help promote an international education that inculcates enduring human values and peace. In this global age, I hope to exert every effort to spread those universal values of the mind and of the spirit that my parents lovingly taught me through the culture and civilisation that I have inherited from them.

ACKNOWLEDGEMENTS

In acknowledgement and appreciation of

Lisa, my wife, without whose love and
loyalty I could not imagine my life, and whose
help and encouragement have been my mainstay
and
My two sons, Salim and Marwan, whose
affection, spirit and creativity inspired
me to write this book